Mr. Marston graduated from Wheaton College, Wheaton, Illinois, in 1928 with a B.A. degree and from Westminster Theological Seminary, Philadelphia, Pennsylvania, in 1932 with a Th.B. He has had a rich and varied experience as a home missionary, pastor and evangelist. At present he is serving as field representative for Westminster Theological Seminary. In this capacity he has occupied many pulpits in this country. While this is Mr. Marston's first book, he has written a number of tracts and pamphlets, several of which have been translated into foreign languages.

THE
VOICE
OF
AUTHORITY

THE

VOICE

OF

AUTHORITY

George W. Marston

The Presbyterian and Reformed Publishing
Company
1960

To my wife,
Pauline Ramsay Marston

CONTENTS

PREFACE

How does one decide what is true or false, what is right or wrong, what is good or bad? Every man has a standard in matters of truth and conduct. This is his Voice of Authority. This voice is found either in God or in man. While God in His Word has revealed Himself to be this Standard, man, as a result of the fall, has usurped this position for himself. Broadly speaking, the consistent Christian recognizes God as his Voice of Authority while the non-Christian has given this authority to man.

The purpose of this book is twofold: to show the inadequacy of man to serve himself in this capacity and to set forth God's claims to be the Voice of Authority.

Is the Voice of Authority God or man? The author was impressed with the importance of this question as a student at Westminster Theological Seminary while attending the course in Apologetics conducted by Dr. Cornelius Van Til. Some twenty-five years in the ministry, both as a preacher and as a personal worker, have deepened his convictions as to the importance of this question. There can be no consistent acceptance of the full-orbed Christianity of the Bible unless one rejects man and accepts God as his Voice of Authority.

The author wishes to thank two of his former professors for reading the manuscript and for their valuable suggestions in regard to its improvement: namely, the Rev. R. B. Kuiper, Professor Emeritus of Practical Theology, Westminster Theological Seminary, President Emeritus, Calvin Seminary, and Dr. Cornelius Van Til, Professor of Apologetics, Westminster Theological Seminary.

This book is written to the glory of God and with the prayerful hope that God may use it to bring many to recognize Him as the Voice of Authority and thus to accept His Son as their Savior, also to find certainty concerning questions of eternal significance, and to be able to speak with certainty concerning matters of truth and conduct which men must face in daily living.

GEORGE W. MARSTON

February 1960.

FOREWORD

God or man?

That is the perennial and incomparably the most important question confronting each man and the entire race of men.

The Bible tells us that our earliest ancestors answered, "Man." That constituted their first sin. Hence all the subsequent sin and misery of mankind.

The identical question comes to us today.

To reply "God," is to acknowledge the Bible as God's self-revelation and to accept that revelation, its miracles, mysteries and paradoxes included, as the infallible norm of truth and goodness.

To reply "Man," as is done in most educational institutions and even from many supposedly Christian pulpits, is to flounder about in the morass of subjectivism, skepticism, agnosticism and atheism. That answer accounts for the demoralization of today's social, political, economic and religious life.

Not everyone who replies, "Man," carries that reply through to its logical conclusion. Nor does every one who replies, "God," abide by that reply with unerring consistency. Yet, basically every human being is dominated in his thinking, willing and feeling by one or the other of those replies.

The Reverend George W. Marston has entitled his discussion of the aforenamed issue "The Voice of Authority." He contends, and rightly so, that every man finds his Voice of Authority either in God or in man. And he upholds unswervingly God as the Voice of Authority and rejects uncompromisingly man as the Voice of Authority.

He has dealt with that profound subject in so lucid and forthright a way that even he who runs may read.

May God use this little volume to unstop the ears of many that they may discern the divine Voice of Authority and, in complete submission, say: "Speak, Lord, for thy servant heareth."

R. B. KUIPER
Professor Emeritus of Practical Theology,
Westminster Theological Seminary;
President Emeritus of Calvin Seminary

THE
VOICE
OF
AUTHORITY

THE VOICE OF AUTHORITY

In the days of the gold rush men used a touch-stone, a fine grained dark stone, such as jasper, to determine the quality of the gold which they had discovered. Today a Geiger counter is used to locate uranium and other precious metals. In baseball the umpire makes the decisions in the contest between the pitcher and the batter. In the court room the judge decides questions of law. In their respective fields the touchstone, the Geiger counter, the umpire and the judge speak with authority.

Is there a Voice of Authority in matters of truth and conduct? Men instinctively recognize the need of such a Voice but they are not agreed as to the identity of this authority. For some this Voice is the conscience. Others have given public opinion this position. For many the church is the Voice of Authority, while others recognize that God alone is qualified to act in this capacity.

As we examine these various views it becomes apparent that basically this authority is either God or man. Even if it be granted that both have a measure of authority, it is still obvious that both cannot be supreme. The other must be subordinate. Which one is the Supreme Authority, the touchstone by which all things must be judged?

Part I

Is Man the Ultimate Authority?

For the majority the Voice of Authority is man. Since God is the Creator and man is the creature, it would seem logical that the creature should recognize his Creator as his Voice of Authority. Why then have the majority given this position to man? The answer to this question is found in the fall of man from the estate in which he was created.

The first three chapters of Genesis contain an account of the creation, man's original estate, his fall and the promise of redemption. They are not to be regarded as myth, fable or allegory but as a God-given revelation of certain historical events. The Lord Jesus alludes to the creation account in Matthew 19:4. The Apostle Paul refers to the fall and sheds light upon its significance in Romans 5:12-19, I Corinthians 15:21 and in I Timothy 2:14. The effects of the fall upon God's perfect work of creation were catastrophic and it is this event which accounts for the present state of man and the world in which he lives.

What happened in the Garden of Eden? God made a covenant with Adam and Eve wherein He promised them eternal life upon condition of perfect obedience and warned them that death would be the penalty if they disobeyed. It is evident from the New Testament passages previously mentioned that in this covenant Adam acted as a representative for the whole human race and that the penalty for disobedience was spiritual as well as physical death. Our first parents, tempted by Satan working through the serpent, disobeyed. The result of this disobedience was the fall.

In reality, this disobedience began when Eve questioned God's authority. On the one hand God had said, "Of every tree of the garden thou mayest freely eat: but of the tree of the knowledge of good and evil, thou shalt not eat of it: for in the day that thou eatest thereof thou shalt surely die" (Genesis 2:16, 17). On the other hand, Satan through the serpent said, "Ye shall not surely die: for God doth know that in the day ye eat thereof, then your eyes shall be opened, and ye shall be as gods, knowing good and evil" (Genesis 3:4, 5). As a creature of God, Eve should have refused even to listen to the Serpent. In so doing, she became the Voice of Authority, sitting in judgment between God and Satan to determine which one had told the truth. The judge who decided against God and for Satan became subject both to the Devil's delusion and God's judgment. Fallen man has acted as though he were God, the Voice of Authority, but in reality he bears the mark of God's judgment. He is subject to death, which is an ever-present reminder that ultimately God is that Voice. However, the true significance of the Grim Reaper is willfully ignored.

The word "fall" aptly describes what happened to man as the result of our first parents' disobedience. He fell from his original estate. He who came from the hand of his Maker perfect in soul and body, made for fellowship with God and to serve the Creator by ruling this world for Him, fell from this position. Not only was man's relationship with God broken but he also became a rebel against God. He who first rebelled by disobeying became a rebel by nature. Fallen man's present relationship to God is evident from Romans 8:7, which reads as follows, ". . .the carnal mind is enmity against God: for it is not subject to the law of God, neither indeed can be." As a result of the fall rebellious men refuse to give God that which is His due as the creator and ruler of the universe. Therefore, men, who are still in this state of rebellion, have refused to recognize God as the Supreme Authority. Instead, they have assumed this position for themselves.

These usurpers have made man the final authority in all matters. They have consciously or unconsciously set up the mind of man as the standard in matters of truth and conduct. As individuals they reason thus: I will only accept that which my mind approves. I cannot approve of that which I cannot understand. Therefore, that which I cannot understand is either untrue or I am not in a position to pass judgment regarding it.

The non-Christian is not always consistent in his allegiance to this principle. He does accept some things which are beyond his understanding. He may even accept views which are contradictory. He recognizes the presence of the mysterious but is unwilling to accept the incomprehensible God or the mysteries of the Christian Faith or the God-given explanation for the mysterious universe in which he lives. The actions of the non-Christian are not always dictated by reason. Sometimes his judgments are intuitive. His choices are influenced by his feelings. He is likely to accept as true and good that which promises immediate relief or enjoyment without stopping to consider the welfare of others or the question of eternal values (Matthew 16:26). In brief, all non-Christians are not rationalists; indeed, many of them are more or less irrational.

Is the existentialist an irrationalist? Existentialism is concerned with the meaning of life, with the conditions and problems which men must face in the course of human existence. Eternity is ignored. Time and history are said to be the dimensions of man's existence. The emphasis is upon the here and now; on the present task of the individual to improve himself inwardly and on the betterment of society as a whole. For the existentialist there are different kinds of truth. For science, truth is embodied in a system of concepts. Religious truth, however, cannot be systematized. It is concerned with matters which are basically above and beyond the reach of reason. Truth in the realm of religion is something which the individual experiences actively and inwardly. (See What is Existentialism?" by William Barrett, *Saturday Evening Post,* November 21, 1959.)

According to this view, religious truth is not objective but subjective. It cannot be defined by a standard, such as the Bible. Neither can it be schematized, reduced to a creedal statement. When one reasons about religion, his reasoning must find its roots in experience, for truth is equated with experience. Religious truth is something which the individual experiences individually, but how does he know if his experience is valid? Even if his experience conforms to that of others, how can he know whether their experience is valid? Existentialism is a form of irrationalism. How can one test the validity of an experience unless he has an objective standard of truth?

It would seem from what has been said that not all non-Christians recognize the intellect of man as the standard in matters of truth and conduct. However, since man is made in the image of God, he is by nature a rational creature. Fallen man cannot ignore or suppress this gift of intellect permanently. Sooner or later the voice of reason must be heard. Its authority must be recognized, at least in some measure. As a result of the fall, however, the non-Christian fails to give the mind its proper place. While some seek to subordinate the intellect to the emotions, most men have gone to the opposite extreme, giving to the mind that place and authority which belongs to God alone. While no man is absolutely consistent in his submission to the voice of reason, most men have either consciously or unconsciously set up their minds as the standard in matters of truth and conduct. All non-Christians assume their own autonomy, and it is unimportant whether this appears in the form of rationalism or of irrationalism.

While the Christian has rejected this principle, namely, that man is his standard, his practice is not always consistent with this rejection. Though his nature has been changed, this change is not complete. While he has repudiated his old nature, he is not always consistent in his repudiation. In some respects he still thinks and acts as though man were his Voice of Authority. From time to time his thinking and conduct must be corrected and brought into a more consistent alignment with the Christian principle that God is the Voice of Authority. The mind as well as the conscience must be educated by Christ through His Word if the Christian is to be consistent in what he repudiates and accepts.

On a number of occasions the Lord Jesus found it necessary to correct the thinking of His disciples.

One such instance took place after His meeting with the rich young ruler. During that interview this most exemplary young man asserted that he had kept the second table of the law from his youth up. Thereupon the Savior exposed his covetousness by challenging him to give up earthly riches for heavenly treasure. If he had to choose between living with his wealth and following the Christ, which would it be? We are told that he went away sorrowing for he had great possessions.

After his departure, the Lord Jesus said to His disciples, "How hardly shall they that have riches enter the kingdom of God! It is easier for a camel to go through the eye of a needle, than for a rich man to enter into the kingdom of God" (Mark 10:23, 25). Thereupon the disciples, filled with astonishment said one to another, "Who then can be saved?" This was their reasoning as revealed by their question: Here is a young man whose virtues are outstanding and whose apparent sin, a love of riches, is common to all men. If he cannot be saved, then no one can. If one so good cannot be saved, then surely the state of all men is one of utter hopelessness.

Christ, the Great Teacher, corrected His disciples with these words, "With men it is impossible, but not with God: for with God all things are possible." In effect the Savior was saying, "You have left God out of your thinking. Not man but God is the Voice of Authority. He alone can say whether or not one

can be saved. Since God has all power, He is able
to save those who are totally unable to save themselves." The Lord Jesus calls His disciples to
consistent Christian thinking, to repudiate man-
made standards of truth and conduct and to use
the divine measuring rod which God has given us
in His Word. In this connection see Matthew 18:1-4,
Mark 10:17-27 and John 6:1-14.

1. GOD IS REJECTED

Those who recognize man as the Voice of Authority and are consistent in their application of this principle reject the God who has revealed Himself in nature and the Scriptures. They do this for two reasons.

God Incomprehensible

In the first place this God is incomprehensible. What does this mean? While man knows certain things about God which He has revealed to him, God in His essence is beyond man's full comprehension. This truth is stated repeatedly in Holy Scripture. Here are several instances. The Psalmist said, "Great is the LORD, and greatly to be praised: and his greatness is unsearchable" (Psalms 145:3). Isaiah the prophet said, ". . . There is no searching of his understanding" (Isaiah 40:28). These words came from the pen of the Apostle Paul, inspired of God, "O the depth of the riches both of the wisdom and knowledge of God! how unsearchable are his judgments, and his ways past finding out! For who hath known the mind of the Lord? or who hath been his counsellor?" (Romans 11:33, 34).

Man cannot fully understand God because He is infinite while man is finite; in other words, while

9

God is unlimited in His being, wisdom, power, holiness, justice, goodness and truth, man is so limited in his being and attributes that God is beyond his full comprehension.

Here are several passages in which certain aspects of God's infinitude are mentioned. Jeremiah 23:24 reads as follows, "Can any hide himself in secret places that I shall not see him? saith the LORD. Do not I fill heaven and earth? saith the LORD." The Psalmist said, "Great is our Lord, and of great power: his understanding is infinite" (147:5). Solomon said, "But will God indeed dwell on the earth? Behold, the heaven and heaven of heavens cannot contain thee; how much less this house that I have builded?" (I Kings 8:27).

Man should need no proof that he is finite, limited not only by the effects of sin upon him and the world in which he lives but also by his very nature as a creature of God. Man, for instance, occupies a limited space while God is everywhere. Great progress has been made in conquering space but no man has yet succeeded in being in two places at once, much less in being everywhere at once. Of particular interest at this point, however, are several passages which stress the limitations of finite wisdom in this matter of understanding God. Job 11:7 reads as follows, "Canst thou by searching find out God? Canst thou find out the Almighty unto perfection?" Job speaks again on this subject saying, "Touching the Almighty, we cannot find him out . . ." (Job 37:23).

Because God is infinite and man is finite there is a qualitative difference between God and man which the telescope of the human mind is not qualified to penetrate. Can a dog understand his master? He may know what reactions his master expects to certain simple commands which he has been taught to obey. However, this does not mean that he has a full, clear knowledge of his master. There are human thoughts and actions which are beyond his understanding because of the essential difference between the nature of a man and a dog. The contrast between God and man is qualitative. The difference is not one of degree but of kind; not merely between a creature which is made in the image of God and one that is not, but between two different kinds of beings, the Creator and the creature.

It is true that God has revealed certain things about Himself to man. The image of God in man is one of the means which God has used for this purpose (Romans 1:19, 20). The fact that man was made in the image of God, however, does not eliminate the qualitative distinction between man and his Maker. This is evident from Isaiah 55:8, 9 which reads as follows, "For my thoughts are not your thoughts, neither are your ways my ways, saith the LORD. For as the heavens are higher than the earth, so are my ways higher than your ways, and my thoughts than your thoughts." Because of the contrast between the nature of God and the nature of man, God in His essence is beyond our understanding.

Because God is incomprehensible, those who are committed to the principle that they will not accept what they cannot fully understand, must logically reject Him. All who do so, however, are not equally consistent in their rejection.

Indeed, some would vigorously object to the charge that they have rejected the one true and living God. They insist that they have simply refused to accept certain things taught in the Bible about Him which seem unreasonable to them. Some, for instance, have rejected the sovereignty of God because it would seem to conflict with man's free moral agency. Others, who think it unreasonable that a God of love should send anyone to hell, have ignored the revelation of God's holiness, righteousness and justice which calls for the punishment of sin.

One cannot reject any of God's attributes without rejecting God! "The attributes of God are not to be thought of otherwise than the aspects of one simple original being; the whole is identical with the parts." They are not "characteristics that God has developed gradually; they are fundamental to His being; the parts together form the whole." (C. Van Til, *The Defense of the Faith*, page 26). While man is still man even though he has lost his arms and his legs, God is not God without all of His attributes. Because of the perfection of His being and the unity of His person, God would not be God if He were lacking any of His attributes. If God is not sovereign, He is not God! If He is limited in His power, He is not God! If He is not holy, righteous, or just, He is not God!

Those who have rejected one or more of God's attributes have, in principle, rejected God. They may not realize what they have done. They may still call upon His name in prayer and seek to walk in outward conformity to His laws but in reality they have given to their own minds the place that belongs to God. These men have dared to sit in judgment upon God; to say what He can or cannot be, what He can or cannot do. The God who is thus rejected in principle, will in time be renounced in practice.

"I will only accept what I can fully understand." The more consistently men apply this principle as they seek to comprehend the one true God, the more consistent they will become in their rejection of Him because He is incomprehensible. However, because man is so constituted that he must have a god, those who are committed to this principle have been forced to reconstruct a god whom they can understand. Every time they reject some truth, which God has revealed about Himself, because it is beyond their full understanding they replace it with a product of their own imagination. The fruit of their labors is a god whom man can comprehend, a finite god whom man has created. Being limited in his being and wisdom, this god knows nothing that man could not know and solves no problems that man could not solve. Because he is limited in his holiness and justice, this god is not really offended by sin nor does he demand everlasting punishment for sin. This god of limited power did not create, neither does he rule the universe or man. Since he himself is subject to the laws of nature, this god cannot perform miracles. He cannot reveal himself to man except through the laws of nature. In brief, he resembles a kindly old man who wishes everyone well but is powerless to do more than wish.

This concept of God finds no support in nature or the Scriptures. This invisible image is wholly unable to meet the needs of man because he does not exist. He cannot even blot out the Reality whom his makers would escape seeing. Though they may be unwilling to acknowledge it, they know that this idol which their minds have created, is not God! Will thinking men insist on rejecting a God whom they cannot comprehend when this is the alternative?

Man's Autonomy Threatened.

In the second place, those for whom man is the Voice of Authority, have rejected the creator and ruler of the universe because He threatens their autonomy.

While God is incomprehensible, there is much that men may and do know about Him. He has revealed Himself in nature. The Psalmist said, "The heavens declare the glory of God; and the firmament sheweth his handiwork. Day unto day uttereth speech, and night unto night sheweth knowledge. There is no speech nor language, where their voice is not heard" (Psalms 19:1-3). God has also revealed Himself in man whom he made in His own image (Genesis 1:27), in the Person of Christ whom Paul describes as the image of the invisible God (Colossians 1:15), and through the prophets and apostles in Holy Scripture.

It is true that, as a result of the fall, the revelation in nature has been marred and that contained in man has been corrupted. It is also true that man lost his ability to read the divine blueprint accurately, and yet it is evident from Romans 1:18-23 that man konws enough about God to render his thinking and conduct inexcusable.

Because fallen man is in a state of rebellion against God, because he is intent upon maintaining his own autonomy, he rejects the God who has revealed Himself as the sovereign of the universe. This God would replace man as the Voice of Authority. He would rule man. Therefore fallen man represses the knowledge which he possesses. He is like a small boy with his fingers in his ears but still he hears some of that which he would escape hearing. In the day of judgment he must give an account for that which he knows.

2. PARADOXES REJECTED

Those who make man their supreme authority in matters of truth and conduct, if logical, must also reject the mysteries of the Christian faith, the paradoxes which are found in the Bible. What is a paradox? R. B. Kuiper has made the following comment in answer to this question, "A paradox is not, as Barth thinks, two truths which are actually contradictory. Truth is not irrational. Nor is a paradox two truths which are difficult to reconcile but can be reconciled before the bar of human reason. That is a seeming paradox. But when two truths, both taught unmistakably in the infallible Word of God, cannot possibly be reconciled before the bar of human reason, then you have a paradox."

If God says two things are true which man cannot harmonize with his finite mind, the Christian will accept them as true, simply because God says so. Those for whom the mind of man is the highest authority refuse to do this. Because they have rejected the God who is beyond finite understanding and also because they refuse to accept anything which they cannot fully understand, they must, if logical, refuse to admit the existence of a paradox of this nature. They are therefore compelled to reject or to modify any paradoxes of this type which they find in the Bible. Such statements are for them irrational.

The Trinity

Those who cannot accept a paradox must reject the doctrine of the Trinity. The word "Trinity" is not found in the Bible but the writers of Holy Scripture do speak of the "Godhead" and the Westminster Shorter Catechism summarizes the teaching of the Bible on this subject in these words, "There are three persons in the Godhead; the Father, the Son and the Holy Ghost; and these three are one God, the same in substance, equal in power and glory." This statement is based upon such Scripture passages as: I Peter 1:2; John 1:18; John 1:1, 14; Romans 9:5; Hebrews 1:8; Acts 5:3, 4; Deuteronomy 6:4; Mark 12:29; I Corinthians 8:4; I Timothy 2:5; John 10:30, 15:26; Matthew 28:19; II Corinthians 13:14.

"We cannot accept the doctrine of the Trinity. How can one God exist in three persons?" This is the view of those for whom man is the final authority in matters of truth. A scientist in Rochester, New York, while discussing the Trinity with a minister, asked this question, "Can you tell me how one plus one plus one can equal one?" The minister replied, "No, but one times one times one does equal one." The answer was clever but it ignored the basic problem. This mystery, which lies at the very heart of the Christian faith, is one which the finite mind cannot solve. This truth must be accepted by faith. It must be accepted as true because God, who is the Truth, has declared it to be true.

A number of problems must be faced by those who reject the doctrine of the Trinity. For example, if there are not three persons in the Godhead, how can the writers of Holy Scripture say that the Father is God, that the Son is God and that the Holy Spirit is God? Church history has recorded the failures of men who attempted to answer this question. Moreover it is impossible to disclaim the Trinity without rejecting the Biblical doctrine of salvation. While the various members of the Godhead work together in every aspect of salvation, certain aspects of this work are attributed primarily to each of the three. For instance, the Father is said to have chosen a people for Himself, the Son came to earth to redeem those whom the Father chose and the Holy Spirit applies to them the redemption which Christ purchased for them.

Without the Triune God there can be no salvation in the Biblical sense of the word.

If Jesus Christ were not the eternal Son of God, His death could not have atoned for the sins of His people. If He were an ordinary man, He himself was in need of a Savior. An ordinary man has sins of his own for which an atonement must be made. If by some miracle, he were a perfect man, it is conceivable that, if God were willing to accept him as a substitute, he might have atoned for the sins of one man.

However, in order to atone for the sins of all His people, there had to be something extraordinary about His Person. It was the Person of Jesus Christ, the God-Man, which made His atoning work acceptable to the Father. It was the divine nature in the Person of Christ which gave infinite worth to the suffering and death of His human nature on Calvary's Cross. Because of the infinite worth of His Person, this one death of Christ actually atoned for the sins of all of His people (Matthew 1:21; 26: 28).

If the Holy Spirit were not God, how could He apply to the people of God the redemption which Christ purchased for them? The Prophet Ezekiel had a God-given vision in which he saw himself in an open valley filled with dry bones, all that remained of many men slain in some great battle. As he gazed upon this grim scene, the Spirit of the Lord said to him, "Son of man, can these bones live?" And he answered, "Lord God, thou knowest." Then in this vision Ezekiel saw the God of infinite power perform a miracle, recreating the men who had died here long ago. Before his very eyes the bones came together, then sinews and flesh came upon them, skin covered them, God breathed upon them and they lived and stood upon their feet, an exceedingly great army.

We are not concerned now with the central significance of this vision recorded in the thirty-seventh chapter of Ezekiel or with the scope of its application but simply with the fact that we have here, not only an allusion to but also a graphic illustration of the Holy Spirit's work as He begins to apply to men the redemption which Christ purchased for them. As a result of the fall, those for whom Christ died are spiritually dead. Before they can perceive and appropriate the redemptive work of Christ a miracle must take place. They must experience a spiritual resurrection (John 3:3, 6, 7; 11:25, 26; Ephesians 2:1; Titus 3:5; I John 3:14).

Only the power of God can produce this necessary change. It is God the Holy Spirit who does this work in the lives of those for whom Christ died. It is He who raises them from their state of spiritual death and gives them spiritual life. He gives these men new hearts, new wills, new dispositions and new desires. Then men begin to hate the things they formerly loved and love the things of God towards which they were formerly hostile or indifferent. Those spiritual faculties corrupted by the fall are also restored by the Spirit of God. Blind eyes are opened. Deaf ears are unstopped. Thus men are enabled to see themselves as sinners and Jesus Christ as the only Savior. The persuasive power of the Holy Spirit attends the preaching of the gospel. By these various acts the Holy Spirit persuades and enables men to embrace Jesus Christ, freely offered to them in the gospel. In the light of these facts, it is folly to deny the deity of the Holy Spirit. If He were not God, no man would experience salvation.

The Two Natures of Christ

If one refuses to accept paradoxes he must, if logical, also reject the Lord Jesus Christ. The teaching of Holy Scripture concerning Him is concisely summarized in the Westminster Larger Catechism by the following statement, which is found in the answer to Question 36, "The only Mediator of the Covenant of Grace is the Lord Jesus Christ, who being the eternal Son of God, of one substance with the Father, in the fullness of time became man, and so was, and continues to be, God and man, in two distinct natures, and one person forever." This statement is based upon the following passages of Scripture: I Timothy 2:5; John 1:1, 18; 10:30; Galatians 4:4; John 1:14, Isaiah 7:14; 9:6; Luke 2:52; Colossians 2:9, Philippians 2:5-11.

The paradox is not found in the Person of Christ as such. The question is not, "How can Jesus Christ be both a divine person and a human person." While the Lord Jesus has two natures, he is one Person. If one were to graft the branch of a peach tree onto an apple tree, the result would be not two trees but one tree with two kinds of branches. The tree would still be an apple tree. This illustrates in a limited way the relationship between the Person of Christ and His two natures.

Jesus Christ is one Person. This Person is the

eternal Son of God, the second Person of the Trinity. Some nineteen hundred years ago, this Person added to His divine nature a human nature; in other words, a true body and a reasonable soul. While the Person of Christ is eternal, His human nature began at a definite time, conceived by the Holy Ghost and born of the Virgin Mary. This nature never existed as a distinct person. It had no personality of its own but from the moment it began to exist, God brought this nature into vital union with Himself. "Just as the body, with its wonderful constitution of organs, nerves, senses and passions, has no personality of its own, but during its entire life in the womb, grows into the personality of the soul, so the human nature of Christ never for an instant had a separate personal existence of its own, but, from the instant of its conception, grew into the eternal personality of the Son of God" (A. A. Hodge, *Commentary on the Confession of Faith*, page 195). The personality of the Lord Jesus Christ is not human but divine. While He has two natures, His Person is divine.

The paradox concerning the two natures of Christ is found in the relationship which exists between these two natures. What is this relationship? The Westminister Confession of Faith describes it in these words, ". . .two whole, perfect and distinct natures, the Godhead and the manhood, were inseparably joined together in one person, without conversion, composition, or confusion" (see Chapter 8, Section 2). The following Scripture passages give warrant for this statement: Luke 1:35; Colossians 2:9; Romans 9:5; I Peter 3:18; I Timothy 3:16. According to the Bible then, the two natures of Christ are not only inseparably united but also always distinct. His human nature did not become divine nor did His divine nature become human. The two natures were not blended into a third nature which is neither divine nor human; and while the writers of Holy Scripture consistently attribute to the Person of Christ that which is true of either nature, they never attribute to one nature that which is true of the other. To quote Dr. A. A. Hodge, "It is said that God—i.e., the Person who is a God—gave his blood for the church; but it is never said that his divinity died, or that his humanity came down from heaven" (*Commentary on the Confession of Faith*, page 196).

Dr. Hodge pinpoints the paradox in these words, "It is impossible for us to explain philosophically how two self-conscious intelligences, how two self-determined free agents, can constitute one person. Yet this is the precise character of the phenomenon revealed in the history of Jesus" (page 195). This learned man did not reject this paradox. Because he recognized the Bible as the Word of God and because the God of the Bible was his supreme authority in matters of truth, he was willing to accept truths contained in the Bible, truths which he could not harmonize, truths which were beyond his finite understanding.

What does the founder of Barthianism, which is

sometimes called "The New Orthodoxy," do with
this paradox? While Barth repeatedly says that Jesus
Christ is very God and very man, what does he
mean by this statement? On the one hand Jesus
Christ is said to be wholly God; on the other hand,
in Jesus of Nazareth, God becomes man.

For more than 1500 years the Church has recognized that the relationship between the two natures
of Christ constitutes a paradox. The teaching of
Holy Scripture on this subject was formulated by
the Council of Chalcedon in 451. Barth, however,
rejects the two natures of Christ and finds his
paradox in a Jesus whose one nature was at once
both human and divine. For Barth this is the
paradox, that one who lived on earth a truly human
life should at the same time be the divine Son of
God. (See *"The Barthian Theology and the Man of
Today,"* by John McConnachie, pp. 75, 315 f.).

While this certainly sounds pardoxical, it is not
a paradox in the Christian sense of the word. As
previously defined, a paradox consists of "two truths,
both taught unmistakably in the infallible Word of
God, which cannot possibly be reconciled before
the bar of human reason." God does not say in His
Word that Jesus Christ is wholly God, neither does
He tell us that in Jesus of Nazareth God becomes
man. Holy Scripture does not describe Jesus Christ
as a person whose one nature is both human and
divine. This is rather the paradox of irrationalism.
One nature cannot be both human and divine. This

is a real contradiction. Barth's view of Jesus Christ would seem to imply; that God was wholly incarnate, and that in some sense God actually suffered and died upon the cross.

Opponents of Barth have been accused of ignoring statements made by Barth which would refute their charges against him. The truth of the matter is that Barth contradicts himself. As previously indicated, he believes that Jesus Christ is wholly God and that in Jesus of Nazareth, God becomes man. These views are self-contradictory. Because he is an irrationalist, Barth believes that opposites are true, that truth contradicts itself. His teachings must always be evaluated in the light of this basic principle. Whenever Barth contradicts himself, he must be held responsible for both sides of the contradiction.

What does the rationalist do with this paradox concerning the relationship between the two natures of Christ? If he is consistent he will reject either the divinity or the humanity of the Savior.

In apostolic times certain men, called Gnostics, denied that Jesus Christ had a real human nature. The Apostle John considered this to be a very serious error for he said, "Hereby know ye the Spirit of God: Every spirit that confesseth that Jesus Christ is come in the flesh is of God: and every spirit that confesseth not that Jesus Christ is come in the flesh is not of God: and this is that spirit of antichrist, whereof ye have heard that it should come;

and even now already is it in the world" (I John 4:2, 3). Why did John insist that a true prophet must teach that Jesus Christ is come in the flesh, in other words, that He had a true human nature? Here is the answer. He had to have a true human nature to act as a substitute for His people; to keep the law for us and to pay the penalty for our law breaking (Romans 5:19; Galatians 4:4, 5; Hebrews 2:14, 17).

The so-called "modernists" of today would solve this paradox by rejecting the divinity of Christ. They regard Jesus as only a man, a great teacher of religion, a perfect example, but only a man. However, if Jesus were only a man then, as we have already shown, He could not be the Savior. Indeed, He cannot even be accepted as a great man, a peerless teacher or the perfect example. According to all historical documents which record the life of Christ, this Jesus made claims for Himself which were absurd for one who was only a man. For instance, to His disciples, gathered in the upper room for the Last Supper, He said, "I am the way and the truth and the life: no man cometh unto the Father but by me." When a great multitude came with swords and staves to the Garden of Gethsemane to seize Jesus, Peter drew his sword to defend his Master. Whereupon Jesus said, "Put up thy sword. . .thinkest thou that I cannot now pray to my Father, and he shall presently give me more than twelve legions of angels? When Caiaphas, the high priest, placed Jesus under oath and asked Him if He were the Christ, the Son of God, the Lord Jesus replied, "I am." If Jesus were only a man and made such claims as these, He was either an impostor or an imbecile.

To deny either the divinity or the humanity of Christ is to reject the true historic Jesus, the only one who is qualified to save men from the temporal and the eternal consequences of sin. Think twice before rejecting this paradox! What will it profit a man if, by insisting on the supremacy of his intellect, he loses his soul?

3. THE MIRACULOUS REJECTED

If the mind of man is the standard of truth, one cannot stop with the rejection of the paradoxes which are found in Holy Scripture. He is also compelled to discard the miraculous because he has rejected the key which makes the miraculous possible and reasonable. Thus we find men rejecting the following doctrines of Holy Scripture: the inspiration of the Bible, the virgin birth, the miracles, the resurrection of Jesus Christ and the promise of a resurrection in the last day. Such men reason this way, "I cannot accept the Bible as the Word of God because the various books so clearly bear the imprint of the personality of their writers," for example, the style of Peter's epistles is different from the style of those written by Paul. The same kind of thinking also leads to the rejection of the various miracles which we have just mentioned. Men say, "We don't see how such events could occur in a universe in which everything operates according to the laws of nature."

The key which these men have rejected is the God who has revealed Himself in nature and the Scriptures, the God of infinite power. When the Sadducees ridiculed the idea of a resurrection, the Lord Jesus said to them, "Ye do err, not knowing the scriptures, nor the power of God." The God of whom Christ spoke was the God of creation. He created the worlds by the word of His power. At His command the universe began to exist. He suspended the earth in space and hung the stars in the firmament above. Even as a man has the power to start and to stop and to control the operation of the machine which he has made, so the God of creation and providence has the power to work through the laws of nature or to set them aside and perform miracles. The virgin birth, the resurrection of Jesus Christ, or the resurrection of all men in the last day are not difficult for the God who created the universe.

This God has the power to communicate His will to men through the prophets and apostles in whatever way He desires. In some instances God gave His spokesmen messages to deliver and enabled them or others to remember and to record them infallibly. Most of Holy Scripture, however, was given by God the Holy Spirit through the personalities of the prophets and the apostles as they thought and wrote. These men did not function as scribes or stenographers. They made full use of their personalities. Their writing was the result of investigation, research and/or thinking (Luke 1:1-3). It was the Holy Spirit who, without suppressing their personalities, miraculously guided the prophets and apostles in these labors, preserving them from error and enabling them to make known through their writings the truths which God would have revealed. Because of the Holy Spirit's miraculous guidance, the fruit of their labors is the infallible Word of God (II Timothy 3:16, II Peter 1:20, 21).

Here is a Latin proverb which sheds light on the subject at hand, "*Ex nihil, nihil fit.*" What does this mean? There can be no effect without an adequate cause. That the Bible is the Word of God and that the various books bear the imprint of the writers' personalities poses no problem for the Christian. The infinite God has revealed Himself to be the adequate cause which has produced this effect. Since we recognize the divine Author to be the God of all power, there is nothing unreasonable about the method or the result. However, this is not the case with those for whom man is the standard of truth. Because they have renounced the God of infinite power, they must also reject the Bible as the Word of God, and vice versa. They know of no cause adequate to produce this effect. A finite God would lack the power to communicate his will to men through a human personality without having the message so distorted or corrupted that it could not be called the Word of God. While Barth maintains that the Word of God comes through human error, failure and contradiction, the infinite God, according to His Word, has not used this method of communication and a finite God could not.

What is the attitude of such men toward the Bible? Some consider it to be the best book on religion ever written by men. Its authority rests solely upon this recognition. Progress in the field of religion would outdate some things taught in this book. The time might even come when the Scriptures could only be regarded as a historical document which, like the covered wagon, indicates a stage in man's progress.

For Barth and Brunner the Bible is only potentially the Word of God. They would not identify the Word of God with the Scriptures. The Book becomes the Word of God only when God speaks to the individual through it. (See *Christianity Rightly So Called* by Samuel G. Craig, pages 203-204). What do they mean by this? Let us suppose that two men were to read the same chapter for their devotions and that each one has an idea come to him that helps him with some problem that he is facing. Perhaps these two different ideas came to these two men as they were reading the same verse. Now, according to this view neither the book, the chapter nor the verse is the Word of God but rather the idea which came from reading the verse. God speaks to individuals individually through this book but what He says to one does not have authority for another. The Book is not an objective standard in matters of truth and conduct. Neither the individual, the state nor the church has a God-given objective standard by which they may pattern their conduct or judge the actions of men.

Among those who reject the Bible as the Word of God are some who recognize that the Bible contains the Word of God. At first glance these men might seem to have a God-given standard in matters of faith and practice but what do they mean by this statement? Simply this, that while some of the Bible is the Word of God, much of it is not. Certain truths are to be found in the Scriptures, truths which God has revealed in nature, truths which for the most part are to be found in other religions. These truths and perhaps others have been discovered by the writers of the Bible. Such truths must, however, be winnowed from the chaff of fiction, fable, legend, symbolism and history in which they were embedded and preserved by these writers of the past.

This work of separating the chaff from the wheat calls for experts but even such men are not always agreed as to their findings so the question is this, "If the Bible only contains the Word of God, how can we be certain as to what is the Word and what is not?" The identity of the Word, the acceptance or rejection of certain statements as the Word of God, becomes a matter of opinion. Therefore the Bible cannot be regarded as an authoritative standard. It is man who determines what is the Word of God. It is man who determines what is his final authority in matters of truth and conduct. In reality, man is his own authority.

Those who have rejected the miraculous cannot evaluate properly the Jesus of history and Scripture. Further evidence to support this statement is found in the fact that some of the miracles recorded in the New Testament were designed of God to shed light on His person and work.

The virgin birth marked Him as the promised Messiah. In the Scriptures of the Old Testament, God gave His people a prophetic picture of the Savior so that they would recognize Him when He came. One aspect of this picture was His virgin birth. The uniqueness of His birth identified Jesus as the Promised One (Isaiah 7:14; Matthew 1:22, 23). The miracles performed by the Lord Jesus led men to recognize Him as Christ the Prophet. Those who witnessed His feeding of the five thousand said, "This is of a truth that prophet which should come into the world" (Deuteronomy 18:18; John 6:14; 7:40, 41;4:19-26). The miracles of Christ were also used of God to attest His divinity. When the Lord Jesus stilled the tempestuous waves of the Sea of Galilee those who were in the ship came and worshipped Him saying, "Of a truth thou art the Son of God."

A sixfold significance is attached to the resurrection of Jesus Christ by the writers of Holy Scripture. This event proves His divinity, assures the Christian of his justification, illustrates the change which the believer experiences in regeneration, sanctification and glorification, gives promise of a life hereafter, proves the possibility of a resurrection in the last day and warns men to prepare for the judgment (Romans 1:4; 4:25; 6:4-6; Colossians 3:1, 2; John 14:19; I Corinthians 15:12, 20; Acts 17:30, 31). If the Lord Jesus did not really rise from the dead, then every significance attached to this event is meaningless.

It is apparent from what has been said thus far that the consistent application of the principle under consideration leads men logically to reject the basic tenets of Christianity, strip the supernatural from the Bible, reduce Jesus Christ to a mere man and reconstruct a Christianity so radically different from historic Christianity that it really has no right to the name.

4. AGNOSTICISM

The same type of thinking which leads men to reject the one true God, the paradoxes found in the Bible and the miraculous elements of Christianity, also leads to agnosticism; to the view that man cannot know what is true or false, right or wrong, good or bad. If one is consistent in applying this principle that man is the ultimate authority in matters of truth and conduct, then agnosticism is inevitable because man is inadequate to act in this capacity.

That man must make judgments is not to be denied. This God-given responsibility must be exercised many times a day. However, while the mind must act as a judge, it cannot be the standard by which the judgment is made. Questions in the realms of truth and conduct must be judged by some objective standard. Paul said that the Jews in Berea were "more noble than those in Thessalonica, in that they received the word with all readiness of mind, examining the scriptures daily, whether these things were so" (Acts 17:11). The Scriptures were the objective standard which the Bereans used in judging Paul's teachings concerning Jesus Christ.

What is true in the realm of the spiritual must also be true in the secular realm. Man must be the judge but he cannot be the standard by which the judgment is made. The judge or jury is not the law but simply the person or body whose work is to interpret and apply the law to the case at hand. It cannot be denied that some of the standards by which men make judgments are man-made but unless these standards are also an expression of the law of God as revealed in nature or stamped on the heart of man in his creation by God, they are erroneous and will in time be discarded or corrected. In reality, the objective standard which men should use in making judgments is the revelation which God has given to men in nature and the Scriptures. This standard alone is infallible and authoritative.

Intellectual Agnosticism

This is evident when one considers the alternatives. What happens when the mind of man is made the ultimate authority in matters of truth and conduct? If two men disagree, by what standard will their difference be judged and settled? Is public opinion to be the standard? Any student of history knows that the majority have been wrong frequently. At one time it was commonly thought that the earth was flat, until quite recently most men thought that it was round like a globe, but now the globe concept concerning the shape of the earth has been modified somewhat. Is one man to be accepted as this authority or are a number of men to be recognized as the authority in their respective fields? Can any man be an infallible standard? What man can say, "I have examined all the facts. There is no possibility of error in my conclusions. I am positive that my position will still be recognized as correct in the next century." Why do textbooks on science have to be replaced? Someone discovers that the expert has made mistakes or that his knowledge on a certain subject was inadequate.

If neither public opinion nor the expert is qualified to serve as the authoritative voice, then every individual becomes his own standard, but what man is qualified to serve himself in this capacity? If neither the majority nor the expert are infallible, how can the ordinary man regard his own judgment to be infallible in matters of truth and conduct? Obviously he neither can nor does, so he recognizes that his conclusions are only personal opinions. How does this lead to agnosticism? If the mind is the standard of truth and every mind is equally ultimate, if two men disagree and there is no higher authority to whom they can go, their difference cannot be settled. They cannot know which one is right and which one is wrong. They cannot know whether a certain view is true or false. They can only conclude that, while all men have a right to their opinions, no one can speak with authority. No one can say, "I know." Logically we must be agnostics.

Moral Agnosticism

This kind of thinking also leads to Moral Agnosticism. If the mind of man is the ultimate authority in matters of conduct then, when men differ as to what is right or wrong, there is no voice to speak with finality in this realm either. The man who accepts the Ten Commandments and the man who rejects them have an equal right to their opinions. Are free love and marriage both morally right? Are management and labor subject to certain moral laws in their relations with one another or is expediency their only concern? Does the individual have a right to own property or should the state be the owner? Should free enterprise or government control be the practice in industry?

If there is no objective standard in the realm of human relationships, then men should also be agnostic in regard to moral issues. For this reason some men have refused to take a stand on the above and similar questions. Others, however, motivated by selfish desires, self-determined expediency and a lust for power, have taken an immoral stand and attempt to use force to gain their ends.

Religious Agnosticism

Religious Agnosticism is also a logical result if the Voice of Authority resides in the individual. No one can speak with certainty concerning religious matters. True, the Bible is a book on religion but there are other books and each individual must weigh the opinions found in them, but his conclusions can only be his personal opinion. Granted, Jesus Christ was a great religious leader but there were other leaders whose opinions differed from His. Each individual must weigh the views expressed but his conclusions can be nothing more than his personal opinion. No man can say with certainty what is true or false in the realm of religion. Logically, men who are committed to the principle under consideration should be agnostic in this realm also.

Because some ministers are basically committed to this principle they do not preach with a Voice of Authority. Instead, they feed their flocks upon the opinions of men. This diet, however, does not satisfy because men instinctively listen for a voice that will speak to them with authority in matters of religion. For this reason some have drifted away from the church entirely while others seek churches where this voice is still heard.

In their search for the missing voice some unenlightened Protestants have mistakenly turned to the Roman Catholic church. Here one finds a voice of authority but what is that voice? While Rome does recognize the Bible to be the Word of God, in practice she has substituted a fallible church for the infallible Word as her ultimate authority. The voice is not that of God, but of man.

Those who search for the true Voice of Authority will find it in churches where the Bible is recognized as the infallible Word, where the minister is conscious of the fact that as God's spokesman he must preach the whole counsel of God; setting before men God's way of salvation by grace through faith in Christ alone, giving men God's solution to the problems of life, and speaking with authority on such subjects as heaven, hell and the judgment. Such preaching will glorify God, change men and satisfy the hearts of those who by the grace of God look for the Voice of Authority.

5. IRRATIONALISM

Is agnosticism the end of the road? Sad to say, it is not. If one is consistent in applying the principle under consideration, the result is Irrationalism. If the finite mind is the ultimate authority in matters of truth, the intellectual agnostic cannot even say, "I know that I cannot know what is true or false." He can only express his opinion. If the mind of man is the touchstone in the realm of conduct, then the moral agnostic cannot even say, "I know that I cannot know what is right or wrong." He can only express an opinion. If every individual is his own standard in matters of religion, then the religious agnostic cannot say, "I know that I cannot know that God is, or that Jesus Christ is the God-Man and the only Savior, or that there is a judgment day coming in which I must answer to the God whom I have ignored and denied." This man may say that there is no hell but how can he prove it? This is only his opinion. He may be wrong.

This kind of thinking does violence to the very nature of man. Man, the rational creature, becomes lost in a sea of irrationality. Man, the moral creature, becomes lost in a morass of immorality. Man, who is instinctively religious, is unable to find either certainty or satisfaction in religion. Those who follow this principle to its logical conclusion are forced to repudiate what they affirm and to affirm what they repudiate. Thus the atheist in his foxhole prays to the God he says does not exist. This is irrationality! Institutions of higher learning that promote this kind of thinking by the type of instruction given in their departments of philosophy, education, science and religion have perverted the purpose of education. Irrationalism can never be the goal of education.

These are the logical results of man's setting up his own mind as the Voice of Authority in matters of truth and conduct. As Jeremiah the prophet said, "O LORD, I know that the way of man is not in himself: it is not in man that walketh to direct his steps."

Part II

God Is the Voice of Authority

If the Voice of Authority is not to be found in man, then it can be found only in God.

As the Lord Jesus Christ stood before Pilate in the Judgment Hall, He said, "To this end was I born and for this purpose came I into the world, that I should bear witness to the truth. Every one that is of the truth heareth my voice." Then Pilate said unto Him, "What is truth?" Is there a Voice of Authority in matters of truth and conduct? Pilate's answer as revealed by his question was "no." He had followed the implications of non-Christian thinking to their logical conclusion. He was completely agnostic. On the other hand, the reply of the Lord Jesus to the same question was "yes." It is evident from His statement which is before us that there is such a thing as truth, that truth has been revealed and that some men know some truths.

Perhaps someone has this question in mind, "Who knows the truth and in what sense is the

43

truth known?" It should be obvious that God knows the truth in a sense that man does not. He knows it completely while man's knowledge of the truth is incomplete. What shall we say about man's knowledge of the truth? Briefly, this. The Christian knows the truth in a sense that the non-Christian does not. He knows its spiritual significance. The non-Christian has a greater knowledge of the truth than his actions would indicate for he often represses the truth which he possesses, refusing to act upon it. There are many truths in the realm of nature which God has revealed to all. Every man has a real but incomplete knowledge of these truths (I Corinthians 2:9-14; Romans 1:19-25; 2:14, 15).

1. THE GOD WHOM CHRIST REVEALED

The truths to which Jesus Christ came to bear witness are manifold. That He came to reveal God to His people is pertinent to the subject under discussion. The Lord Jesus came to earth to add to that revelation of God which He had previously given in nature and through the Old Testament prophets. It is evident from the following passages that both nature and the Scriptures were His organs of revelation in the Old Dispensation (John 1:1, 2; Romans 1:20; Psalms 19:1, 2; 97:6; I Peter 1:10, 11). During His earthly sojourn, the Son revealed God to man. John said, "No man hath seen God at any time; the only begotten Son, which is in the bosom of the Father, he hath declared him." Matthew tells us that on a certain occasion, the Lord Jesus made this statement while addressing a great throng, ". . .neither knoweth any man the Father, save the Son and he to whomsoever the Son will reveal him." In the upper room, when Philip said to Jesus, "Show us the Father and it sufficeth us," the Savior replied, "Have I been so long time with you, and yet hast thou not known me, Philip? He that hath seen me hath seen the Father; and how sayest thou then, show us the Father?"

The God whom Christ revealed in nature, in

the Scriptures and in Himself is a personal God who has all the attributes of personality and has them in infinite perfection. This God is unlimited in His being, wisdom, power, holiness, justice, goodness and truth. He created the universe by the word of His power. He sustains and rules the world in which we live. This God is the supreme authority in all matters of truth and conduct. Why does He qualify as this standard?

The Standard of Truth

God is qualified to serve as the Standard of Truth because He is Truth. This attribute is as essential to the nature of God as the lungs in man are to breathing. A God without truth would not be God! The omniscient God is infinite in His knowledge of the truth. Nothing is unknown to Him who is the author and revealer of all the truths which this universe contains. God's knowledge of the truth is comprehensive. There is no possibility that anyone will ever discover that God has made a mistake. He is infallible. In Him man has an infallible Standard of Truth.

The Standard of Conduct

God qualifies as the Standard of Conduct because He is holy and righteous.

God is holy. The vision which Isaiah saw in the temple was designed to impress him with the holiness of God. As the prophet gazed upon that scene he heard the seraphim cry one to another, "Holy, holy, holy, is the LORD of hosts: the whole earth is full of his glory." Because God is holy He is utterly sinless. He is absolutely pure. When Isaiah measured himself by this standard he said, "Woe is me! for I am undone; because I am a man of unclean lips and I dwell in the midst of a people of unclean lips: for mine eyes have seen the King, the LORD of hosts."

God is righteous. The Psalmist said, "For the righteous LORD loveth righteousness" (Psalms 11:7). When we say that God is righteous we mean that it is His nature to do that which is right, that God is always just in all His dealings with His creatures, that He is morally perfect in all His actions. Abraham based his plea for the deliverance of Sodom upon the righteousness of God for he said, "Shall not the Judge of all the earth do right?" He lost his plea on the same grounds. Because God is righteous He refused to overlook the sins of Sodom. Therefore God destroyed that wicked city (Genesis 18:23-19:28). It should be noted in passing that because God is righteous He loves righteousness and requires it of all men.

Because God is holy and righteous He cannot sin. While God's attributes are unlimited, He is limited by His attributes. While God is not limited by anything outside Himself, He is limited by His own nature. The Almighty cannot contradict Himself. God is restricted by the very fact that He is unlimited in His being, wisdom, power, holiness, justice, goodness and truth. Because He is unlimited in His power, He cannot create a stone bigger than He can lift. Because He is holy and righteous, He must be absolutely pure and morally perfect in all His actions. The holiness and righteousness of God are mirrored in the moral law and pictured in the perfection of Christ's perfect conduct. In this God we have the perfect Standard of Conduct.

Circular Reasoning

Those who recognize God as the Voice of Authority in matters of truth and conduct reason this way. God is truth. If God has declared a certain thing to be true, then I will accept it, even though I cannot understand it or reconcile it with other truths. God is righteous. His standard of righteousness must be my pattern of righteousness. I must conform to God's standard even though my old nature rebels and public opinion disapproves.

An objection arises at this point. Someone says, "Aren't you reasoning in a circle?" Some would have us think that circular reasoning is always bad and must be avoided at all cost. However, it is impossible to avoid this type of reasoning. The validity of any statement can only be established by an appeal to some authority such as the Bible, a law of nature or man's reason. The man who would prove his point states his authority and then says, "This is true because my authority says so."

This is circular reasoning. This type of reasoning lies behind every statement. If the circle is not consciously completed, it is presupposed. If one says, "Two plus two is four," he presupposes an authority for this statement. His authority may be a textbook but behind that book are the laws of nature which have to do with mathematics. If the non-Christian were to support this statement consciously and consistently he would reason thus: A law of nature is my authority. Two plus two is four because this is a law of nature. Since God is the author of the laws of nature, the Christian who thinks consistently will begin and end this circle with God. (See Rousas J. Rushdoony, *"By What Standard,"* pages 139, 140 for further development of this subject.)

In reality, since the ultimate authority must be God or man, one can only reason in one of two circles. He may begin with self and end with self, or begin and end with God. The self-centered thinker reasons this way. "My mind is my standard of truth. What I decide to be true is true. Any statement not acceptable to me is not true." This is circular reasoning. On the other hand, the God-centered thinker reasons this way. "God is truth. Whatever God says is true. If God declares a certain thing to be true, I must accept it, even though I cannot understand it or harmonize it with other truths." This is also circular reasoning. Those who have made man their final authority in matters of truth and conduct are self-centered thinkers. They are committed to the first circle in their reasoning. The second circle of reasoning is the mark of those who recognize God as the Voice of Authority.

The non-Christian is basically, though not consistently, a self-centered thinker. He sets himself up as the judge and summons the infinite God, as well as his fellow men, to appear before this judgment bar to answer for their conduct. In dealing with God this judge reasons thus. This is my idea of justice. If God doesn't conform to my idea, He is not a God of justice. This is my idea of love. If God has permitted war and its devastations, He is not a God of love. On the other hand, the Christian, though not always consistent, is basically a God-centered thinker. He recognizes that the infinite God cannot be expected to conform to the multiplicity of men's ideas on such subjects as love, goodness, justice, holiness and truth. The only way in which men can expect to attain unity in their views on such subjects is to seek to bring their thinking in line with what God has to say on these matters. Therefore the Christian recognizes God as the Voice of Authority in all matters of truth and conduct.

Commitment to this standard compels the Christian to interpret events in a manner which is consistent with the nature of God as expressed by His attributes. This principle constrains the Christian to say, "Since God is good, if He has done or permitted a certain thing to be done, then this must be compatible with His goodness." While men often do things for an evil purpose, God has a good purpose in permitting these things to happen. This is evident from the story of Joseph (Genesis 37-50).

Faced with the horrors of war, the Christian reasons this way. God is love. Whatever God does or permits must be compatible with His love. While war and its devastations are the result of sin and an expression of God's judgment upon the nations, it is also true that God's reasons for permitting such things must be compatible with His love for His people. In Romans 8:28 God has given the Christian this assurance. "All things work together for good to them that love God, to them who are the called according to his purpose."

Who can deny that injustice is all too common? Many deplore the manner in which Russia has dealt with captive nations behind the Iron Curtain, but what individual has not experienced some form of injustice in the common relations of life: in the family, in business or society? Why has a God of justice permitted these acts of injustice? Again the Christian must seek an answer which does not conflict with the nature of God and he finds his answer in the nature of God. Thus we hear him say, "God is just. Whatever God does or permits must be compatible with His justice. Therefore God must have a reason compatible with His justice for permitting the unjust actions of men. That reason may be unknown to me; indeed it need not be known to me, but it must be consistent with the nature of God and He is just." However, if a man must have a reason, let him consider this one. Man's injustice to God, the failure of individuals and nations to render to God that which is His due as the creator and sovereign of the universe, has merited all the injustice which we have experienced at the hands of one another.

2. GOD HAS REVEALED
HIS TRUTH AND RIGHTEOUSNESS

Since God is the Voice of Authority, this question arises, "Where may men learn of Him? Where has He revealed His truth and righteousness?" The answer in brief is this, "In nature and the Scriptures."

God has partially revealed His truth and righteousness in nature. The Psalmist said, "The heavens declare the glory of God; and the firmament sheweth his handiwork. Day unto day uttereth speech, and night unto night sheweth knowledge. There is no speech nor language where their voice is not heard" (Psalms 19:1-3). The righteousness of God is revealed in the laws of nature, especially through the moral law which was written in the heart of man in creation, and also in God's providential dealings with His creatures (Romans 2:14, 15; Psalms 145:17).

Why did God create man? To people the earth and to rule the world to the glory of God (Genesis 1:28). In obedience to the creation mandate, man's task is to discover the truths which God has revealed in nature, to accept God's interpretation of these truths, to use them for their God-intended purposes and to rule the world according to the principles of righteousness which God planted in him and gave to him by special revelation. This was so from the beginning. God spoke to our first parents in the garden, telling them that He had created fruit trees, fowls and beasts to provide them with food. God also told them that they were to care for the garden, to dress and keep it. Man was also called to accept God's interpretation of the significance of the tree of the knowledge of good and evil.

Great progress has been made in the discovery of truths revealed, for instance, in the fields of science, art and industry. Great basic principles have been discovered which men use as touchstones as they continue their search for truth in their respective fields. Sad to say, however, many of the men who have made these discoveries fail to recognize that they have discovered God's truths. They, therefore fail to grasp the full significance of these truths. In some cases, certain truths have even been perverted by man's failure to use them for their God-intended purposes.

Because man is made in the image of God he has discovered in himself the principles of righteousness. Although this revelation has been marred by the fall, man still has a general knowledge of these principles. This is evident from the similarity between the Code of Hammurabi and the Ten Commandments. Even though fallen man is in a state of rebellion against God, even though he lacks the basic motives and ability to apply these principles, man has been both influenced and restrained in his conduct by them. Therefore he is accountable to God for his conduct (Romans 1:18-2:15).

God has also revealed His truth and righteousness in the Bible. We need not fear that the revelation in nature and the Scriptures may contradict one another because God, who is the author of both, does not contradict Himself. The revelation in nature, however, is lacking in two respects. Because it was marred by the fall it is fallible and must always be interpreted in the light of the Scriptures. This revelation is also incomplete. Since it was given before the fall, it has nothing to say about God's plan of salvation. In the Bible, which is the Word of God, we have a perfect and a complete revelation of those things which God would have us believe concerning Him and those duties which He requires of us. This Book is therefore man's touchstone in all matters of faith and practice.

3. OBJECTIONS TO THE BIBLE ANSWERED

In the nature of the case, those who deny that the Bible is the Word of God do not consider it authoritative. If they are correct in their view of the Bible, it cannot be regarded as an infallible authority in any realm. The scope of this chapter will not permit a thorough answer to this objection. Those who are concerned with this subject are referred to *Thy Word is Truth*, written by Dr. Edward J. Young, Professor of Old Testament at Westminster Theological Seminary in Philadelphia, who deals with this question in a thorough and a scholarly manner. It will challenge the thinking of honest doubters who are broadminded enough to consider the evidence.

Here are some assertions which should stimulate further study on this subject. The Bible claims to be the Word of God (II Peter 1:21; II Timothy 3:16). While there are internal and external evidences which support this claim, ultimately the acceptance of the Bible as the Word of God depends upon the inward testimony of the Holy Spirit (I Corinthians 2:10, 11).

Concerning the Bible's Claims

As has been previously indicated, there are internal and external evidences which support the

Bible's claim to be the Word of God. Here are some samples of this evidence.

The historical accuracy of the Bible is attested by the findings of archaeology. It has been said that the Bible cannot be accepted as an infallible book because it contains historical inaccuracies. However, the archeologist's spade has uncovered evidence which has vindicated the historical accuracy of the writers of Holy Scripture in case after case. The reader who wishes to pursue this subject is referred to Donald Wiseman's *Illustrations from Biblical Archaeology* and J. A. Thompson's (*Archaeology and the Old Testament, Archaeology and the New Testament* and *Archaeology and the Pre-Christian Centuries*).

A question arises at this point. Must we wait until the spade has finished its work before the Bible can be accepted as the infallible Word of God? Never! While the Christian is glad to hear that in case after case the writers of Holy Scripture have been vindicated, and while we are confident that the complete accuracy of the original manuscripts will be fully verified, if not in time then certainly in eternity, we need not wait until all the problems concerning the texts at hand have been solved. We can accept the Bible as the infallible Word now because the God of infinite wisdom and knowledge, who already knows what men have yet to discover, has declared it to be so.

The indestructibility of the Book also gives support to the Bible's claim to be the Word of God.

Isaiah the prophet said, "The grass withereth, the flower fadeth: but the word of our God shall stand forever." True, individual copies of the Bible may be destroyed but the efforts of men to eliminate this Book have always failed and always will. Kings have ordered every Bible seized and burned. Philosophers have sought to destroy the Scriptures with logic and ridicule. Voltaire predicted that, as a result of his attack, within a hundred years the Bible would be a forgotten book. Today, while Voltaire and his writings are all but forgotten, the Bible is a "best seller."

Consider the transforming power of the Book. The Holy Spirit has used it to transform the lives of individuals and nations (Hebrews 4:12; Romans 1:16). An atheistic trader, seeing that the natives in a certain African village possessed Bibles, said to the chief, "You don't believe in that Book, do you?" This was the chief's reply, "If it were not for the Bible, you would have been in our cooking pots long before this." Contrast the nations where this Book is read and its precepts practiced with those where it is not. The fruit of the Book attests its divine authorship. It is the Word of God.

The Bible contains many prophecies which have already been fulfilled. The Old Testament prophets foretold future events, not in the vague, hazy, general terms employed by fortune tellers but with minute detail. There were, for instance, over three hundred prophecies concerning the first

Advent of the Messiah which were made hundreds of years before the Lord Jesus came to earth. Every one of these prophecies was minutely fulfilled by the Savior. These prophets were very conscious of the fact that their message was from God. They spoke with a "thus saith the Lord." The fulfillment of these prophecies attests their claim. Since only God knows the future, fulfilled prophecies attest the claim of the Bible to be the Word of God.

Consider the unity of this Book. In reality, this is not a book but a library consisting of sixty-six books written by more than thirty different authors over a period of some fifteen hundred years. Three different languages are found in the Bible. The racial and cultural backgrounds of the writers are marked by variety. These men wrote under varying circumstances. They had no opportunity to get together beforehand and map out the Book; to agree on policy; to adopt principles which would guide them in their writing. The unity of these books is most remarkable. The various writers are in absolute agreement. They do not contradict but supplement one another in their message. These books are so unified in their teaching that we think of them as one book. Where else could one find a library consisting of sixty-six volumes, written by thirty or more authorities in a given field, where all the writers are in absolute agreement? How can we account for the unity which we find in the Bible? Here is the answer. Behind the minds and pens of these writers was the mind of the Almighty God. The unity of the Book attests its divine authorship.

While these proofs are accepted by many because they seem to be reasonable and while they are a source of comfort and strength to the believer, the truth must be stressed that their validity rests ultimately upon the fact that they are a part of the God-given revelation which the Holy Spirit uses to convince men that the Bible is the word of God.

We have said, for instance, that the indestructibility of the Bible indicates that the Book is God's Word. Many have accepted this statement because the evidence given in its support seems reasonable to them. A few, however, will say, "You have given us a possible explanation for the Bible's indestructibility throughout the ages but there may be other explanations. How can we be sure that this one is correct?" If the mind of man is the Voice of Authority, there is no answer to this question. The reasonableness of the evidence is a matter of personal opinion. However, those for whom God is the Voice of Authority have the answer. This is our reply, "We know that this is the correct explanation of the Bible's indestructibility because God says so. Isaiah the prophet said, 'The grass withereth, the flower fadeth: but the word of our God shall stand forever'."

In reality then, these proofs are valid because they are based upon the Word of God. Thus, our authority for accepting the Bible as the Word of God is God Himself.

Concerning the Meaning of the Bible

One more objection remains to be considered. Some say, "Since there are so many different opinions as to what the Bible teaches, how can we use it as a standard in matters of faith and conduct?" Who would deny that some parts of the Bible are hard to understand: for instance, certain prophetic passages. The language is figurative or symbolic and the meaning of a prophecy is often hidden until after it has been fulfilled. Most of the Bible, however, is written in plain prose. True, in order to understand the spiritual significance of the truths stated, one must have spiritual discernment; but given this discernment, the Christian should be able to understand what God is saying in at least the plain prose passages in Holy Scripture. Indeed, with the illumination of the Holy Spirit promised in I Corinthians 2:12-16, the careful student of the Bible should also be able to discover the meaning of many of the more difficult passages.

There are three basic rules which must be observed by those who would ascertain the meaning of any kind of literature. If the Christian will observe these rules in his study of the Bible, he should be able to know in most cases what God is saying through the prophets and apostles.

First the words must be taken in their plain

historic sense; in other words, in that sense in which they were used in that period of history in which they were written. Words have a definite meaning. Black is not red or yellow or brown. One does not have a right to change the meaning of a word in order to give weight to his views. The so-called "modernists" who engage in this practice are guility of intellectual dishonesty. When the writers of Holy Scripture speak of the resurrection of Jesus Christ they are not talking about the immortality of His soul. Neither does the word "atonement" mean "a vicarious example of suffering." The Scriptures were translated from the Greek and Hebrew by linguistic experts; men who were qualified to transmit the meaning of the words used in these manuscripts, to give us the sense in which they were used by the writers.

The reader of one of these translations, commonly called a "Version," does, however, face this problem. These men translated the Bible into the language of their day and, since some words have come to have a different meaning with the passing of time, this fact must be kept in mind as we read the various versions. The reader must ascertain the sense in which the words were employed in the particular period in which that version of the Bible was produced. Some of the words in the King James Version are used in a different sense than they are today; for instance, the word "careful" as used in Philippians 4:6 means "to be full of care or anxiety" and the word "prevent" which is found in I Thessalonians 4:15 means "to precede." This factor must also be considered as one seeks to discover the historic meaning of the words contained in a particular version.

The second rule is that the text must be interpreted in the light of the context. According to this rule, the meaning of a word or a phrase or a verse is also to be ascertained by the setting in which it is found. The meaning has to be in harmony with what the writer is saying in the passage. Why is the context important? Words have several meanings. Such words, for instance, as leaf, ring and note may be used in several different senses. However, when one of these words occurs in a sentence, its setting, in other words its context, indicates the sense in which the writer has employed the word. This principle must also be applied by those who would interpret the Scriptures aright.

Why do men get such conflicting ideas from the Bible? In many cases it is because they have ignored this basic principle just mentioned. Instead of trying to discover what the God-inspired writer of Holy Scripture is saying in a given passage, they go to the Bible only to find support for their own views. In order to find this support, they take words and phrases and sentences out of their context and make them say something quite different from what the prophet or apostle is really saying in that passage. Here is an extreme example of this malpractice. A tract written by an atheist contains this statement, "The Bible says, 'There is no God'." What the Psalmist really said was this, "The fool hath said in his heart, there is no God" (Psalm 14:1). When one takes a word or a sentence out of its context, he loses or perverts its meaning. The text must be interpreted in the light of the context. If more men would follow this rule there would be greater unanimity regarding the teaching of Holy Scripture.

There is a third rule to be observed. Scripture must be interpreted in the light of Scripture. This rule is based upon the unity of the Book. It recognizes the Bible as the Word of God. It assumes that God is self-consistent, that what He says on a certain subject in one part of the Bible is bound to be in harmony with what He says elsewhere in this Book on the same subject. This rule also recognizes that God has not made a complete statement on any one subject in any one place in the Bible. In this Book God has spoken on such subjects as heaven and hell, peace and war, marriage and divorce, the obligations of Capital and Labor, but the deposits of truth on each of these subjects are to be found in various places.

This rule—that Scripture must be interpreted in the light of Scripture—has both negative and positive implications.

No one passage may be interpreted in a way which will bring it in conflict with the teaching of other passages in the Bible. Because the Bible is the Word of God, Scripture cannot contradict Scripture. True, as we have already seen, there are paradoxes in Holy Writ which contain truths that seem to be contradictory but aside from these, unless the interpretation given a certain passage is in harmony with the total teaching of the Bible, it cannot be correct. Here is a case which illustrates this principle. John 3:17 reads as follows, "For God sent not his Son into the world to condemn the world but that the world through him might be saved." Some would interpret this verse to teach that God intends to save all men. This interpretation, however, must be rejected because it conflicts with the teaching of such passages, for instance, as John 3:36, which contains the statement, "He that believeth on the Son hath everlasting life: and he that believeth not the Son shall not see life; but the wrath of God abideth on him." The conflict between this interpretation and the words of Christ as contained in Matthew 25:46 is even more apparent. In speaking of the judgment, the Lord Jesus pictures the final destiny of those who were found wanting in these words, "And these shall go away into everlasting punishment."

In other words, the best commentary on the Bible is the Bible. If one seeks light on a certain passage, he will find it in other passages which deal with the same subject. He will first gather and then put together the teaching of Holy Scripture on this subject even as a boy fits together the various parts of a jigsaw puzzle. If the seeker should find certain truths which do not seem to fit together, he simply sets them aside until he finds the other truths which are necessary to bridge the gap. If the searcher should fail to find them, he may assume that the inadequacy is in himself. Such failure, however, seldom occurs. Because the Bible is God's Word, its teachings will not contradict but will supplement one another. In most instances the fruit of such labors will be a composite picture of what God would have us know concerning the subject in question.

4. THE MIRACLES ACCEPTED

God is the supreme authority in matters of truth and conduct. How does one apply this principle as he studies the Bible? The student of the Word will accept what God has said in His Word. This means that he will accept the Bible as the Word of God and thus will accept the miracles recorded in the Book. These matters present no problem to the God-centered thinker. He recognizes that the God who created the worlds by a simple command, the God who has revealed Himself in nature and the Scriptures, has the power to work through the laws of nature or to set them aside and perform miracles. The Almighty has the power to use men as scribes or to speak through their personalities. In revealing His will to men through the prophets and apostles, He did both. The Almighty One has the power to perform miracles: to prepare a great fish to swallow Jonah, to produce the human nature of Jesus Christ by the virgin birth and to raise Him from the dead on the third day. Since God has all power, there is nothing unreasonable about such miracles. We will simply accept the claims of the God of truth. These things are true because God says so.

Those who recognize God as the Voice of

Authority will not stop with an acceptance of the miracles recorded in Holy Scripture, they will seek and accept only God's interpretation of these miracles.

What, for instance, is God's interpretation of the miraculous healing of the palsied man recorded in Mark 2:1-12? This miracle was not designed to indicate that Christ was a prophet, though He was the prophet foretold by Moses in Deuteronomy 18:18, and the ability to perform miracles was a mark of a true prophet. Nor is this merely another example of the Savior's compassion (Mark 6:34). Before He performed this miracle, the Lord Jesus gave it this significance, "But that ye may know that the Son of man hath power on earth to forgive sins (he saith to the sick of the palsy), I say unto thee, arise, take up thy bed, and go into thy house." It is evident from Daniel 7:13, 14 that the title "Son of man" does not indicate the humanity but rather the divinity of the Lord Jesus Christ. It is clear, when one weighs the Savior's words in the light of the narrative as a whole, that Christ was saying in effect, "The miracle which I am about to perform is a sign to you that I, being divine, have power to forgive sins."

To accept any other explanation of this miracle is to ignore or reject the significance given it by the Savior Himself. Obviously, He is the Voice of Authority. Spokesmen for both the "old" and the "new" modernism seek to persuade men to accept something less than God's interpretation of the miracles recorded in the Bible. Those who recognize God as the Voice of Authority will reject such attempts.

We cannot be satisfied with the view that the virgin birth was designed to teach that God's revelation to man begins in a mysterious way. This is not God's interpretation of this miraculous event. The Voice of Authority, through the prophet Isaiah and the apostle Matthew clearly indicates that this miracle was designed of God to identify Jesus Christ as the promised Messiah (Isaiah 7:14; Matthew 1:18-23).

What is the meaning of Christ's resurrection? Some would have us believe that this event signifies that God's revelation to man ends in a mysterious way. This, however, is a fabrication of men. Through the apostle Paul, God tells us, for instance, that this miraculous event was a divine attestation to the truth that Jesus Christ is the eternal Son of God (Romans 1:4). Note again the sixfold significance which God has given this event (see page 33).

God is the Voice of Authority! It is apparent that if one is consistent in his application of this principle to the Bible, he will accept not only the miracles but also God's interpretation of them.

5. THE PARADOXES ACCEPTED

Since God is infinite and man is finite, the student of the Word must expect to find in Holy Scripture things which are beyond his understanding. God said through the prophet Isaiah, "My thoughts are not your thoughts, neither are your ways my ways, saith the LORD. For as the heavens are higher than the earth, so are my ways higher than your ways, and my thoughts than your thoughts." Because God is our sovereign and we are His subjects the student must submit his mind to God's will as revealed in His Word and accept the mysteries of the faith, the paradoxes, without question. The paradox of the Trinity and the two natures of Christ are recognized by Christians and the truths involved are accepted simply because God has declared them to be true. There are, however, other paradoxes which some Christians have refused to accept because they have failed to apply consistently the principle before us: namely, that God is the Voice of Authority in matters of truth and conduct. These are also essential to the system of truth revealed in Holy Scripture.

God is Sovereign; Man, a Free Moral Agent

One of these paradoxes embraces these seemingly contradictory statements: God is sovereign; man is a free moral agent. Perhaps these statements need to be amplified. On the one hand, the Bible clearly teaches the sovereignty of God, in other words, that the God who created the universe rules this world according to His own predetermined plan. While men often do things which are contrary to God's revealed will, which is set forth in Holy Scripture, no man does that which is contrary to His secret will which is unfolded in the events of history both great and small. The nature of the sovereignty of God is evident from such passages as: Daniel 4:35; Ephesians 1:11, 22, 23; Genesis 50:20. On the other hand Holy Scripture recognizes man as a free moral agent. While man is limited in his actions by his nature and his environment, he truly makes his own decisions and is accountable for all his actions. In the Bible man is addressed as a free moral agent. The various aspects of this statement are supported by the following references: I Corinthians 2:14; Acts 19:23ff; Joshua 24:15; Isaiah 55:6, 7.

These paradoxical truths, which are taught separately in different passages, are also found side by side in the same passages. Joseph said to his brothers, ". . .ye thought evil against me; but God meant it unto good, to bring to pass as it is this day, to save much people alive" (Genesis 50:20). In order to grasp the significance of this statement, one must interpret it in the light of the narrative which begins with the thirty-seventh chapter of Genesis. Briefly, and without detail, the facts are these. The brothers of Joseph, moved by jealousy and hatred, sold him to men who took him to Egypt to serve as a slave. God, however, had a good purpose in permitting this evil incident. This was simply the first in a series of events whereby the God of providence made provision for Jacob, his sons and their families during the seven years of famine which were coming.

Because the sovereign God controls the actions of men, He was able to bring this to pass. At the same time, it must also be recognized that these men acted as free moral agents. They freely chose to do the things which God had purposed for reasons which were pleasing to themselves. The wife of Pharoah's captain was moved by spite to have Joseph cast into prison. The King's butler was primarily concerned with pleasing his master when he made known Joseph's God-given ability to interpret dreams. Pharoah was thinking of the welfare of his people when he installed Joseph as Prime Minister with orders to prepare the country for the seven years of famine which were predicted by the King's dream as interpreted by Joseph. It was a desire to see his brother Benjamin which first moved Joseph to compel his brothers to return again and to bring this loved one with them. Gratitude to Joseph constrained Pharoah to give good land in Egypt to Jacob and the other sons. Thus, the family through which the promised Messiah was to come, was preserved and cared for during these years of jeopardy. Here we see man, the free moral agent, freely and unconsciously doing the will of the sovereign God. How can this be?

On the Day of Pentecost, God-inspired Peter accounted for the crucifixion in these words, "Him, being delivered by the determinate counsel and foreknowledge of God, ye have taken, and by wicked hands have crucified and slain" (Acts 2:23). In these words, this event is attributed to both God and man. On the one hand, Peter tells us that the crucifixion of Christ was not an accident but the fulfillment of God's eternal plan, an act of the sovereign God bringing to pass that which He had planned. On the other hand, this apostle charges the Jews with having put to death their promised Messiah. He describes their actions as "wicked" and holds them responsible. Accountability implies free moral agency. How can this be?

As Peter spoke to that group of Jews who assembled in Solomon's Porch of the temple after the healing of the lame man, he told them that in putting Jesus to death, they had ignorantly fulfilled all that God had foretold through the prophets concerning the suffering of Christ (Acts 3:17, 18). In so doing, they acted as free moral agents. They were not constrained in their actions even by a knowledge that Jesus was the Christ and that He must die for the sins of His people. Their reasons for crucifying this Jesus were radically different from God's purpose in permitting this to come to pass. In this event, God's sovereign will was done by men who were free moral agents. How can this be?

Those who have set up their own minds as the touchstone of truth are forced to reject this paradox. In doing so, some deny that man is really a free moral agent. They seem to regard man as a machine that blindly does the will of God, or as a puppet on a string. But how could God hold such men accountable for their actions? Others would resolve this paradox by rejecting the sovereignty of God. But if God is not sovereign, petition has no place in prayer. If God does not control all things, He cannot answer prayer. Indeed, if He is not sovereign, He is not God!

Those, however, who recognize God as the Voice of Authority, will accept this paradox without hesitation. We cannot understand how God can be sovereign and man can be a free moral agent. Here is something beyond our finite understanding. But since God has declared both to be true, we will accept them as such.

Man is Unable but Accountable

There are some who view man's total inability and man's responsibility as parts of a paradox. Both are taught in the Bible. As a result of the fall, man became totally unable in regard to spiritual matters. In Ephesians 2:1, the Apostle Paul reminds the Christian that his former state was one of death which was not only caused by sin but also characterized by it. Fallen man is not dead physically, mentally, or morally, but spiritually. Even as the physically dead are incapable of any physical actions because they are dead to this physical world, so those who are spiritually dead are by nature incapable of any actions in that spirtual realm called the Kingdom of Heaven. They are as dead men when it comes to matters in this realm. The term "unregenerate" is used to describe those who are spirtually dead. Such men are incapable of any spirtual actions. They cannot change their own nature, right their relationship to God, make themselves the children of God, or do anything in a manner which is pleasing to God. The unregenerate man's total inability in these respects is abundantly evident from the following passages: Jeremiah 13:23; John 6:44; I Corinthians 2:14; 10:31.

At the same time, God holds man responsible for all his actions. Though Eve was deceived by the Serpent and Adam was led astray by Eve, God held our first parents responsible for their disobedience. Though mankind has inherited a corrupt nature from Adam, God holds each one accountable for his sins (Romans 3:23; 6:23). Even though the Savior's betrayal was part of God's eternal plan, Judas was held responsible for his dastardly deed (Luke 22:22). Emphasis must be placed upon the fact that God holds the unregenerate man totally responsible for his inaction and sinful actions in the very realm in which he is totally unable to do that which God requires of him. He who is a sinner by nature must give account of his sins to God, "It is appointed unto men once to die, but after this the judgment" (Hebrews 9:27). He who is unable to respond, is commanded to repent and believe the gospel (Mark 1:15). He who is unable to come to Christ is further condemned by his failure to believe on Him (John 6:44; 3:18). It is therefore evident that man's responsibility is not limited by his ability.

How can a God of justice hold men responsible for their actions in a realm in which they are totally unable? Those for whom man is the voice of Authority reply, "He cannot. One of two things must be true. On the one hand, if man is unable, God cannot justly hold him responsible for his actions. On the other hand, if God justly holds man responsible, he must be able to do that which God requires of him." Let us consider each of these views and trace them to their logical conclusions.

According to the first view, a just God cannot hold man accountable for his actions if man is totally unable. How could Judas, for instance, be held responsible for betraying the Lord Jesus when he only did that which God had decreed from all eternity? How could Judas have done otherwise? This view, however, violates man's free moral agency. If man is not responsible, he is not a free moral agent. Responsibility and free moral agency go hand in hand. The one does not exist without the other. This view reduces man to a puppet on a string.

Advocates of the second view express their judgment in these words, "If God justly holds man accountable for his actions then man must be able to do that which God requires of him." Those who hold this position have been forced to modify the effects of the fall. The result was not spiritual death but only spiritual sickness. Man did not become totally unable in respect to spiritual matters, he was only partially disabled. With the help which God has given to all men the individual is now totally able to do all that God requires of him. Indeed, according to this view, God has given man such power that, in some respects, man now has more power than God. The Almighty must in many vital matters await man's good pleasure. This god, for instance, cannot save anyone until he is willing and ready to be saved. This position does violence to the sovereignty of God. It reduces God to the status of a servant who must await the pleasure of his master.

Are man's total inability and man's responsibility parts of a paradox? If such were the case, those who recognize God as the Voice of Authority would simply say, "Since God has declared man to be accountable for his actions in a realm in which he is totally unable, we must accept both of these truths and recognize that God's action must be compatible with His justice." However, this is not really a paradox. True, man's total inability and man's responsibility are vitally related to at least two paradoxical combinations; namely, the holiness of God and the origin of sin, the sovereignty of God and man's free moral agency, but these truths are not parts of a paradox.

It is logical that God should hold man accountable for his actions even in that realm in which he is totally unable, in spiritual matters. Justice demands it. Similar demands are sometimes made by civil authorities. It is not unusual for the police to require a driver suspected of drunkenness to walk a line. His inability to pass this test does not cancel his obligation to do what he should normally be able to do. Now for the analogy, God created man with the ability to do all that God requires of him. When man fell, he lost his ability but not his obligation. Man's inability in no way destroys his responsibility. God justly demands that man must still do all that God requires of him.

Unconditional Election and the Sincere Offer

Unconditional election and the sincere offer of the gospel are parts of a real paradox. On the one hand, the Bible teaches that, in His eternal counsel, God chose a certain number unto salvation. This number is not small but great. The basis of God's choice was not some good thing which He foresaw in His people but something which lay wholly within God's own inscrutable will. These truths are derived from the following Scripture passages: John 6:37; Revelation 7:9; Acts 13:48; Romans 3:10-12; 8:28-30; Ephesians 1:4, 5; II Timothy 1:9. On the other hand, it is evident from Holy Scripture that there is also a sense in which God may be said to desire the salvation of all men. This desire is not the expression of His secret will but of His revealed will. God has not decreed that all men should be saved but it is His expressed desire that all who hear the gospel should respond to it, that they should come to repentance and faith in the Lord Jesus Christ and that they should come to enjoy the salvation offered through Him in all its fullness. In this connection see: Isaiah 45:22; 55:6, 7; Ezekiel 18:23, 32; 33:11; Matthew 23:37; Luke 13:34; Romans 10:13; II Peter 3:9.

While all the passages mentioned should be carefully examined by those who would investigate the Scriptural basis for the various aspects of these two doctrines, we shall limit our consideration only to as many passages as seem necessary to pinpoint the paradox.

God has chosen certain men unto salvation. There are several passages which clearly teach this truth. Ephesians 1:4, 5 reads as follows, "According as he hath chosen us in him before the foundation of the world, that we should be holy and without blame before him in love: having predestinated us unto the adoption of children by Jesus Christ to himself, according to the good pleasure of his will."

In these words the Apostle Paul tells us that the
Father chose the Christians in Christ before the
world began, that He foreordained us to be His
adopted sons and that the basis for His choice was
not some good thing which He foresaw in us but
a purpose which lay wholly within Himself (see
also II Timothy 1:9).

It is evident from Acts 13:48 that only the elect
truly respond to the gospel. When Paul preached
Christ in the city of Antioch on a certain Sabbath,
Luke tells us that, "as many as were ordained to
eternal life believed." The Lord Jesus accounts for
a limited response to the gospel in these words, "No
man can come to me, except the Father which
hath sent me draw him" (John 6:44). On this same
occasion the Savior also said, "All that the Father
giveth me shall come to me; and him that cometh
to me I will in no wise cast out" (vs. 37). In these
words our Lord indicates that the number of the
elect is fixed and that all the elect, but only the
elect, will be saved.

There is, however, a sense in which God may
be said to desire the salvation of all men. Ezekiel
33:11 reads as follows, ". . .As I live, saith the Lord
GOD, I have no pleasure in the death of the wicked;
but that the wicked turn from his way and live:
turn ye, turn ye from your evil ways; for why will
ye die, O house of Israel?" True, God is here
speaking to the house of Israel but the theocratic
kingdom certainly contained some who were repro-

bate; in other words, some whom God had not chosen unto salvation. It is evident from verses 8 and 9 of this chapter that the word "wicked" must include at least some of this number. And yet God in effect is saying, "I would be pleased if all the wicked in the house of Israel would repent and be saved."

On Tuesday of the Passion Week, the Lord Jesus spoke to a great multitude in the temple. His address on this occasion was climaxed by an indictment of the people of Jerusalem which took the form of a lament. The Savior said, "O Jerusalem, Jerusalem, thou that killest the prophets, and stonest them which are sent unto thee, how often would I have gathered thy children together, even as a hen gathereth her chickens under her wings and ye would not!" (Matthew 23:37-39). In these words the Lord Jesus tells us that He had often desired something which God had not decreed; namely, that the people of Jerusalem would receive Him as their promised Messiah. In other words, He yearned for their salvation, He longed to function as their Messianic King. This desire that men would come to Him for salvation also finds expression in the gospel invitation as set forth in Matthew 11:28-30, "Come unto me, all ye that labor and are heavy laden, and I will give you rest. Take my yoke upon you, and learn of me: for I am meek and lowly in heart: and ye shall find rest unto your souls. For my yoke is easy, and my burden is light."

II Peter 3:9 should also be considered in this connection. In the third chapter of this epistle, Peter is answering a question which troubled the Christians to whom he wrote. Scoffers were asking, "Where is the promise of his coming?" In effect men were saying, "Why hasn't your Lord kept his promise to return? What of the judgment whereof you warned us? We don't believe that these things will ever come to pass." The apostle reassures the Christians with these words, "Forget not this one thing, beloved, that one day is with the Lord as a thousand years, and a thousand years as one day. The Lord is not slack concerning his promise, as some count slackness; but is longsuffering to you-ward, not wishing that any should perish, but that all should come to repentance." In brief, Peter tells his readers that our Lord's seeming delay is not due to slackness but is an indication of his "longsuffering to you-ward."

To whom did Peter refer when he spoke of our Lord's long-suffering to you-ward, or on your account? It is evident from the word "beloved" in verse 8 that the primary reference is to those who are truly God's children. Surely God is long-suffering with His people, even when He chastens us, for our sins deserve much worse punishment. This long-suffering is for our sanctification, our growth in the Christian life. The last clause in verse 9 also sheds light on the people indicated by the word "you." Peter was speaking of mankind as a whole when he said, "The Lord is not willing that any should perish but that all should come to repentance." It is not those who are already saved but the rest of mankind that face the alternatives mentioned here; eternal death or eternal life, which is the fruit of that true repentance which brings men to rest in Christ alone for salvation. The word "you" must therefore include those of whom Peter speaks in the passage which begins with 2:1ff. While these persons may have been professing Christians, who could insist that they were all true believers? Who could doubt that there were even some reprobates among this number?

God is long-suffering, not only with His elect but also with the reprobate. In Romans 9:22 we are told that God "endured with much longsuffering the vessels of wrath." The Apostle Paul speaks to the impenitent in these words, "Despisest thou the riches of his goodness and forbearance and long-suffering, not knowing that the goodness of God leadeth thee to repentance?" (Romans 2:3-5). In these words the apostle indicates that, while God has not decreed the salvation of the impenitent, yet in a sense His goodness, as expressed by His forbearance and long-suffering, is designed to influence such men to repent. This statement would seem to indicate that there is a sense in which God desires and seeks the salvation of the impenitent.

It is true that our Lord delays His return until all His elect are gathered in. Nor is it to be denied that, in His long-suffering, our Father is chiefly concerned with "the blessedness of those whom He has chosen unto salvation, through sanctification of the Spirit, and belief of the truth" (*Matthew Henry's Commentary*). It is also true, however, that the long-suffering of God is occasioned, at least in some measure, by a benevolent desire for the salvation of all. This desire is not the expression of His decretive will, which is revealed in the events of history such as the salvation of individuals, but rather the expression of His preceptive will, which is revealed in Holy Scripture.

For a thorough explanation of the various texts considered in this connection the reader is referred to a pamphlet entitled, *"The Free Offer of the Gospel"* written by Professors John Murray and Ned B. Stonehouse of Westminster Theological Seminary.

The Bible teaches both election and the sincere offer of the gospel. God has chosen certain unto salvation and yet there is a sense in which He may be said to desire the salvation of all. In the gospel God sincerely offers this salvation to all men. When faced with this mystery of the Christian faith, those for whom self is the Voice of Authority are forced to reject at least one part of this paradox.

Some reject the sincere offer of the gospel. Those who take this position say, "If God has chosen a certain number unto salvation, we can't see how He can sincerely offer salvation to all." They maintain that, in such passages as Ezekiel 33:11, Matthew

23:37-39 and II Peter 3:9, we have an expression only of God's desire toward His elect or in respect to the believers to whom the prophet or apostle was writing. However, as we have seen, these passages cannot be so limited.

Most of those who stumble at this mystery, reject the doctrine of unconditional election. Such men reason thus, "We don't see how God can sincerely offer salvation to all men unless all are in a position to accept it." So they make the individual the elector. One sometimes hears election explained in these words, "God votes for you, the Devil votes against you, and you cast the deciding vote." Those who take such a position are forced to ignore such passages as Ephesians 1:4, 5; Acts 13:48; John 6:37 and many more of similar import.

Some Christians, however, seek to harmonize election and the sincere offer of the gospel by removing the unconditional aspect of election. According to this view, God chose those whom He foresaw would respond to the sincere offer of the gospel. His election was conditioned by what He saw men would do with the gospel. Romans 8:29, 30, which reads as follows is quoted in support of this view, "For whom he did foreknow, he also did predestinate to be conformed to the image of his son. . .Moreover whom he did predestinate, them he also called: and whom he called, them he also justified: and whom he justified, them he also glorified." There are two objections to this view.

In the first place this view that God chose those whose faith in Christ he foresaw fails to solve one of the basic problems which must be faced by those who reject this paradox. According to this view, the reaction of each individual is still predetermined. This gives rise to several more problems. Who predetermined each individual reaction which God foresaw? If God did not, then who did? If someone else did, does not this reduce God's predestination to mere divine approval? What kind of god would this be? In the second place, this view cannot be based on Romans 8:29, 30. The word "foreknow" as used here cannot mean simply "to foresee." If it did, then, since God has foreseen all things and has always known all about everyone, this passage would have to teach that God has predestined all to be saved and will surely carry out His plan. Such a conclusion, however, must be rejected because it would bring this passage into conflict with other Scriptures which clearly deny that all men will be saved.

What is the meaning of the word "foreknow" as it is used in this passage? The word "know" is sometimes used in Holy Scripture in a sense which indicates more than mere knowledge. This is evident from Amos 3:2 which reads as follows, "You only have I known of all the families of the earth. . ." While God knew about all the families of the earth, He knew Israel in a special sense. He had chosen them to be His people in a special sense. They were the recipients of His love in a sense that the other nations were not. This passage sheds light on the meaning of the word "foreknow" in Romans 8:29. Dr. Charles Hodge, in his *Commentary on Romans*, indicates that this word involves the idea of selection which was an expression of a special love. In effect the Apostle Paul is saying, "Those whom He had before selected, He also did predestinate to be conformed to the image of His Son. . ."

The Bible teaches both unconditional election and the sincere offer of the gospel. When those who recognize God as the Voice of Authority are convinced that this is the case, they will accept this paradox. True, we cannot harmonize these truths with our finite minds but we will accept them simply because the God who knows all things has declared them to be true.

A Limited Atonement and a Universal Offer

There are two more truths which the mind of man cannot reconcile. On the one hand, the Bible teaches a limited atonement. What is a limited atonement? The word "atonement" means literally "to cause to be at one," in other words "to reconcile." Sin had made a breach between God and man. The holy God was offended by man's disobedience. A just God demanded that the penalty for man's lawbreaking be paid. The Lord Jesus Christ came to effect a reconciliation by satisfying the demands of divine justice in behalf of His people. He redeemed (delivered) them by fully satisfying every demand of the law upon them and every claim of the law against them. During His life he perfectly kept the law for them and by His death He fully paid the penalty for their lawbreaking. This work of atonement was limited, not in respect to its power but as to its design. The atonement was not designed to save all men or to make salvation possible for all men but to accomplish the redemption of those whom God had chosen unto salvation (Matthew 1:21; 20:28; 26:28; John 6:37; 17:6-9). On the other hand, we also find in Holy Scripture a universal offer of the gospel. All men are invited to come to Jesus Christ, to accept Him as their Savior and thus partake of the redemption which He has purchased by His life and death on Calvary's Cross. Here are some of the passages which contain or imply this universal offer: Isaiah 45:22; 55:1, 2, 7, 8; Matthew 11:28-30; John 7:37, 38; Romans 10:13; Revelation 22:17.

Perhaps it would be well to quote several passages which will focus our attention on this paradox.

There are three passages which clearly indicate that the atonement is limited in its design. Before the birth of the Christ Child, the angel said to Joseph, ". . . thou shalt call his name JESUS: for he shall *save his people* from their sins" (Matthew 1:21). As the Lord Jesus gave His disciples that institution which we call the Lord's Supper, He took the cup and said, ". . . this is (represents) my blood

. . . *shed for many* for the remission of sins" (Matthew 26:28). In Romans 8:29, 30, as we have already noted, the Apostle Paul is saying in effect, "for whom He did *select,* He also did predestinate to be conformed to the image of His Son; whom He did predestinate, them He also called, and whom He called, He *also justified.*" The atonement is the ground (basis) for the believer's justification (Romans 3:24). Because the Lord Jesus has atoned for our sins, God the Father has declared us to have satisfied fully every demand of the law upon us and every claim of the law against us. How does this passage teach a limited atonement? Only those whom the Father selected (elected) are the recipients of justification. The atonement, which is the ground of justification, was designed only for these.

The universal offer of the gospel is either stated or implied in such passages as these. Isaiah 45:22 reads as follows, "Look unto me, and be ye saved, *all the ends of the earth:* for I am God, and there is none else." Isaiah 55:6, 7, an exhortation which ends with a promise, is in effect an impelling invitation, "Seek ye the LORD while he may be found, call ye upon him while he is near: Let the *wicked* forsake his way, and the *unrighteous* man his thoughts: and let him return unto the LORD, and he will have mercy upon him; and to our God for he will abundantly pardon." The Lord Jesus gave this gracious invitation to a great throng assembled in the temple on the last day, that great day of the Feast of Tabernacles, "If *any man thirst,* let him come unto me, and drink. He that believeth on me, as the scriptures hath said, out of his belly shall flow rivers of living water" (John 7:37, 38).

A question arises. Someone says, "Before you ask us to face this paradox, please tell us what you do with those passages which seem to teach that Christ has made atonement for the sins of all men. For instance, John 1:29 which reads as follows, 'The next day John seeth Jesus coming unto him, and saith, Behold the Lamb of God, which taketh away the sin of the world.' How can you harmonize this and such passages as I John 2:2; Romans 8:32; John 12:32; I Timothy 2:6; I Corinthians 15:22, with the passages which seem to indicate a limited atonement? Is this another paradox?"

No, this is not a paradox. The two groups of passages can be harmonized. While such terms as "his people," "my sheep," "the church of God" and "many" cannot be interpreted in a way which will reconcile them with a universal atonement, such terms as "the world," "all," and "us all" can be interpreted in a manner which will be in harmony with a limited atonement. If the passages which seem to teach a universal atonement are interpreted in a manner which is in accord with their context and the teaching of Holy Scripture as a whole, they will be found to be in harmony with the passages which teach a limited atonement.

Let us apply this principle to several of the passages which seem to teach a universal atonement. Romans 8:32 reads as follows, "He that spared not his own Son, but delivered him up for us all, how shall he not with him also freely give us all things." At first, glance, this verse might seem to teach that God delivered up His Son for all men but as we examine the verse in the light of its context it becomes apparent that the words "us all" refer to all believers. Paul is speaking to and about believers in this passage. This is the case with a number of the passages.

Another passage which is alleged to support a universal atonement is John 12:32, "And I, if I be lifted up from the earth, will draw all men unto me." Does this passage teach that the crucified Christ will save all men? When viewed in the light of other Scriptures, for instance Matthew 7:13, 14, it becomes apparent that the words "all men" cannot be taken literally for the Lord Jesus will never draw all men to Himself in a saving sense. The context of John 12:32 sheds light upon the identity of the "all men." There were Greeks in the Savior's audience on this occasion. Our Lord's statement was designed to assure them that He would die to save not only Jews but also Gentiles, men of every nationality and class. This is a fact; the Lord Jesus has and will draw all kinds of men to Himself (Revelation 7:9). Now the same thing is true in other passages which seem to teach a universal atonement. If the words "all" or "all men" are taken figuratively, these passages will be in harmony with the Scriptures as a whole.

This is also the case with the word "world" as used in John 1:29 which has already been quoted and in I John 2:2 which reads as follows, "And he is the propitiation for our sins: and not for ours only, but also for the sins of the whole world." Writers of Holy Scripture did not always use the term "world" in a literal sense; see Luke 2:1. Other Scriptures forbid the literal use of the word "world" in the passages before us. Christ has not made an atonement for the sins of all men or all would be saved. Instead the word must be interpreted figuratively to mean "all kinds of men, especially non-Jews." The Apostle John is using the word in this sense to correct the anti-Scriptural idea which was popular among the Jews, that the Messiah was coming only for the benefit of the Jews. John the Baptist was speaking to a Jewish audience when he said, "Behold the Lamb of God, which taketh away the sin of the world." In these words he emphasized the fact that the promised Messiah had come, not only to save Jews but Gentiles as well, all kinds of men.

One more passage should be considered in this connection. In I Timothy 2:6 the Apostle Paul tells us that Jesus Christ, the Mediator, "gave himself a ransom for all." At first glance this verse seems to teach a universal atonement. However, when studied in the light of its context and the analogy of Scripture, it becomes apparent that the world "all" does not mean "all men" but "all kinds or classes of men."

In the first verse of this chapter, Paul urges Timothy and other Christians to pray for all men; not for the church only but for all mankind; not for believers only but for all kinds of unbelievers; not necessarily for every unbeliever but for men of all classes. This apostle then proceeds in verse 2 to mention two classes of men for whom they might be the least inclined to pray, "for kings and for all that are in authority." The church is exhorted to pray, not only for the lowly Christian or for the poor of this world but also for civil authorities. In verses 2 and 3 Paul gives two reasons to support his exhortation to pray for these two classes of men: that we may lead a quiet and peaceable life in all godliness and honesty, for this is good and acceptable in the sight of God.

Why is God pleased that Christians pray for kings and all that are in authority? Paul gives us two reasons in verses 4-6.

Here is the first reason: God "will have all men to be saved, and to come unto the knowledge of the truth." We would not deny that there is a sense in which God may be said to desire the salvation of all men but that is not what the Apostle Paul is saying here. In the light of its context, the sense of Paul's statement is this, "God our Savior is pleased that you pray for these two classes of men because He has willed that all kinds of men or men of all classes be saved." To quote John Calvin's Commentary on this passage, "The present discourse relates to all classes of men, not to individual persons; for his sole object is to include in this number princes and foreign nations."

The second reason follows in verses 5 and 6. In effect the Apostle Paul is saying, "God is pleased to have Christians pray for kings and for all who are in positions of authority because Jesus Christ, the one Mediator who stands between the one God and all kinds of men, has given Himself as a ransom for men of all classes." Since Scripture must be interpreted in the light of Scripture, the word "all" in this verse cannot mean "all men" or it would conflict with our Lord's statement concerning those whom He ransomed. This statement, recorded in Matthew 20:28, is as follows, ". . . the Son of man came not to be ministered unto, but to minister, and to give his life *a ransom for many*." The word "many" can include all classes of men but it cannot include all men.

Both a limited atonement and the universal offer of the gospel are clearly taught in Holy Scripture. This question arises, "Since Christ died only to save those who were chosen of the Father, how can God sincerely invite all men to come to Christ?" Those for whom man is the Voice of Authority have refused to accept this paradox. This refusal has led them to attempt to harmonize these two truths by modifying one or the other.

Some, who recognize that the Bible teaches a

limited atonement, have sought to limit the gospel invitation. This group finds support for its position from such passages as Isaiah 55:1, Matthew 11:28-30, John 7:37, 38, and Revelation 22:17. These invitations are directed specifically to those who are aware of their spiritual need; to those who thirst, to all who labor and are heavy laden and to whosoever wills or desires. Since only the regenerate possess this awareness and since only the elect are regenerate, these invitations are in effect limited to the elect.

That these invitations are conditioned is not to be denied. He who would accept such an invitation must recognize his spiritual need. Nor is it to be denied that they are directed particularly to those who are aware of their spiritual needs. It is also true, however, that such invitations may be sincerely given to all men. This is evident from John 7:37, 38 which has already been quoted. The Lord Jesus gave this invitation to the crowd that thronged the temple on the last day of the Feast of Tabernacles. Certainly there were some in that audience who were unregenerate, even some who were reprobate and yet, in effect, the Savior said to all who were present, "If you recognize your spiritual need and come to me, you will find in me that which will satisfy your need." This was a sincere offer to all who were present.

The universality of the gospel invitation is also taught in other types of passages. There is an implied invitation in the exhortations and promises addressed to the "wicked" and the "unrighteous" in Isaiah 55:6, 7. These two terms are broad enough to include all men for the Apostle Paul said, "There is none righteous, no, not one: . . . there is none that doeth good, no, not one" (Romans 3:10-12). Isaiah 45:22, which has also been quoted, is unique in that the emphasis is solely upon the universal nature of the invitation. To quote Murray and Stonehouse, "There can be no question but that the salvation mentioned in this text is salvation in the highest sense . . . The text is also an invitation and command to all to turn to God and to be saved. The universalism of this command should be apparent from the expression, 'all the ends of the earth.' This is a characteristic Old Testament phrase to designate all nations and peoples. The universal scope is, however, confirmed by the context." See the *"Free Offer of the Gospel"* (pp. 19-20) for further comment on this passage.

Among those who have rejected the paradox which is before us, the great majority have gone in the other direction, seeking to reconcile the design of the atonement with the universal offer of the gospel. Advocates of this view reason thus: since all men are invited to come to Christ, the Savior must have died to make salvation possible for all men. According to this view, the atonement is limited in power but not in design.

Did the Lord Jesus die to make salvation possible

for all men? This view has no basis in Holy Scripture. Passages which would seem at first glance to teach that Christ died to save all men have already been considered but there are none which teach that He died to make salvation possible for all. A question arises, "Why can't the passages which would seem to teach that Christ died to save all men be interpreted to mean that the Savior died to make salvation possible for all men?" There are three objections to this interpretation.

In the first place, even if these passages did teach that Christ died to make salvation possible for all, they would still be in conflict with such passages as Matthew 1:21; 20:28; 26:28 which state that the Lord Jesus died to save a limited number, not all but many.

In the second place, the death of Christ does not make salvation possible for all men. The Bible teaches that, except for children of believers dying in infancy, none will be saved apart from the preaching of the gospel (Acts 16:30, 31; Romans 10:17). Since all men do not hear the gospel in this life and since none will be saved after death, the atonement does not make salvation possible for all men (II Corinthians 6:2; Hebrews 9:27).

In the third place, the atonement is not designed to save all men. True, it is unlimited in its power. The divine nature of the Person of Christ gave infinite worth to the suffering and death of His human nature on calvary's cross. Because of the infinite worth of His Person, His one sacrifice for sin was sufficient to atone for the sins of the whole world. Even as the sun is sufficient for the needs of any number of plants, so the power of the atoning work of the Savior is sufficient for the needs of any number of men. The death of Christ, however, is designed to save a limited number of men, namely, the elect. This is evident, not only from various passages which have already been considered but from the fact that the atonement is described as a ransom in several of these passages. A ransom is not paid merely to make possible the deliverance of all who might wish to avail themselves of it but actually to secure the release of certain individuals. While men may lack the power always to secure the release of those for whom the ransom has been paid, the sovereign God has the power to secure the release of those whom the Lord Jesus Christ has ransomed (John 6:37-40, 44).

Every effort to resolve this paradox has failed. The Bible teaches both a limited atonement and a universal offer of the gospel. Those who refuse to accept what they cannot understand are forced to reject one of these doctrines, to reject part of the Word of God. This is a very serious matter (Revelation 22:18, 19). On the other hand, those for whom God is the Voice of Authority will accept this mystery of the Christian faith, not because our finite minds have solved the mystery but simply because the God of all knowledge and wisdom has said in His Word that both are true.

6. IMPLICATIONS OF REJECTION

The seriousness of rejecting these mysteries of the Christian faith can hardly be overemphasized. Most Christians who do so are consciously or unconsciously motivated by the very same principle which, consistently applied, has given rise to modernism.

A Christian committed to this principle reasons thus, "I do not see how God can be sovereign and man a free moral agent." So he rejects the sovereignty of God. This rejection is marked by inconsistency. He still prays as though God were sovereign. This principle has also led Christians to reject the Biblical doctrines of unconditional election and a limited atonement.

Here is a shocking fact. This same principle, consistently applied, has led the modernist to such conclusions as these. We do not see how a miracle could occur in a universe in which everything operates according to the laws of nature. We cannot accept the Bible as the Word of God because the various books so clearly bear the imprint of their writers' personalities. We must reject the Biblical view that Jesus Christ had two natures because this view cannot be corroborated by experience. How one God can exist in three persons is beyond our

99

comprehension. Thus the consistent application of this principle has led to the rejection of the miracles recorded in the Bible, the inspiration of Holy Scripture, the deity of Christ and the doctrine of the triune God. As we have previously seen, if this principle is applied with thorough consistency, it leads to agnosticism and ultimately to irrationalism.

This principle, namely, that man is the Voice of Authority, is the cancer which threatens the Christian character of the Christian church. It is not to be denied that the reaction to this Voice is more rapid and consistent in churches where dead orthodoxy prevails. Allegiance to tradition rather than the Word of God and an emphasis on outward conformity rather than the necessity of an inward change are the characteristics of dead orthodoxy. Modernism spreads more rapidly in such an environment. Nevertheless, wherever ministers or professors in church colleges or seminaries have accepted the mind of man as the Voice of Authority, the seeds of modernism are present! Such men may sincerely, though inconsistently, reject the implications of their position but in time the consistent application of it will bring them, or others to whom they have taught this principle, to a progressive rejection of the basic tenets of historic Christianity.

There is an old saying to the effect that, if the camel gets his nose in the tent door, he will soon occupy the tent; indeed, he is likely to topple the tent. If the tent is the Church of Jesus Christ, then the camel's nose is this principle that the mind of man is the Voice of Authority. When the camel sticks his nose in the tent door, the moment for decisive action has arrived. Beware of the camel's nose!

7. IMPLICATIONS OF ACCEPTANCE

The implications of accepting God as the Voice of Authority are five.

In the first place, this acceptance implies a regenerate consciousness. Only those whose spiritual natures have been changed are willing and able to accept God as He has revealed Himself in nature and the Scriptures. No longer in a state of rebellion against God, nor desiring to maintain their own autonomy, nor insisting that they will accept only that which they can fully understand, the regenerate readily accept God's revelation of Himself as a "Spirit, infinite, eternal and unchangeable in His being, wisdom, power, holiness, justice, goodness and truth." They not only recognize that God is the creator and ruler of the universe; they also acknowledge His authority over them as individuals, the authority of the creator to rule His creatures. While the regenerate are not always consistent in their recognition of God as the Voice of Authority, those who are unwilling to do so should face this question, "Am I regenerate?"

In the second place, a recognition of God as the Voice of Authority implies that the individual has accepted God as his standard in all matters of truth and conduct.

God has revealed His truth and righteousness in nature and the Scriptures. The revelation in nature, though limited in its scope and affected by the fall, is not to be ignored but the revelation in the Scriptures, though primarily concerned with the salvation of God's people, is perfect and complete. This is the only infallible rule in matters of faith and practice.

The regenerate accept the Bible as the Word of God because of the inward testimony of the Holy Spirit (I Corinthians 2:9-16). While this attestation is supported by internal and external evidences which strengthen our convictions concerning the divine authorship of the Book, our acceptance is based primarily upon the fact that God, our Voice of Authority, has declared the Bible to be His Word (II Peter 1:20, 21; II Timothy 3:16). We accept what we find in Holy Scripture, not because it is reasonable to our finite minds but because the Voice of Authority, the God of all wisdom and knowledge, has declared it to be true. Thus, we are able to accept, not only the simple truths but also the paradoxes, the whole counsel of God, the whole Bible.

How do we apply this principle to life situations? We use the Bible as our touchstone. Isaiah said, "To the law and to the testimony: if they speak not according to this word, it is because there is no light in them" (Isaiah 8:20). All the opinions and practices of men are to be tested by the Scriptures and accepted or rejected on this basis alone.

The third implication of accepting God as the Voice of Authority is conversion. This word describes the reaction of a regenerate man to the gospel. He turns from his sins to God through the Lord Jesus Christ. This turning involves a change of mind and conduct. In conversion a man changes his mind concerning the Voice of Authority. He recognizes that this Voice is not man but God. His conduct is also changed. He no longer seeks to conform to the standards of the world. God is his standard of truth and righteousness and he strives to attain this standard as it is revealed in God's Word.

There are two aspects to conversion: repentance and faith (Acts 20:21; Mark 1:15).

In repentance the individual turns from his sins with godly sorrow because he realizes that in sinning he has offended and grieved God. This same sorrow for sin moves him to turn to God, confessing his sins and seeking God's forgiveness. If we have made man rather than God our Voice of Authority, if we have ignored God's standard of truth and righteousness and have lived by our own, if we have thus worshipped and served the creature rather than the creator, this calls for repentance.

Those who would turn to God in repentance must come to Him through the Lord Jesus Christ, who said concerning Himself, "I am the way, the truth, and the life: no man cometh unto the Father, but by me." In other words, they must accept Him as their Savior. He purchased the pardon we seek from a just and holy God. This pardon is given only to those who believe on Him (John 3:36). Through Christ we receive the adoption of sons (John 1:12; Galatians 4:4, 5). Thus we come into a personal and intimate relationship with the Voice of Authority. He is our Father and we are His children.

The Lord Jesus Christ enables the believer to attain to God's standard of righteousness. He is called "the LORD our Righteousness." Through Him, those who believe on Him are declared to be legally righteous. He has satisfied divine justice on our behalf by fully satisfying every demand of the law upon us and every claim of the law against us. During His life He perfectly kept the law for us and by His death He paid the penalty for our law breaking (Romans 5:15-19; Galatians 3:13). The Savior has sent the Holy Spirit to enable us to make progress in our efforts to conform to the pattern of righteousness which He by His example and precepts has given us through the prophets and apostles (II Corinthians 3:18). When the Lord Jesus Christ returns He will perfect the work begun in this life. We who are now perfect in our legal righteousness will then be also morally perfect.

On the one hand, it is the Voice of Authority who points men to the Son saying, "This is my beloved Son, in whom I am well pleased; hear ye him." On the other hand, the Son has declared Himself to be the way to the Father for He said, "No man cometh unto the Father, but by me." Before a man can fully accept God as the Voice of Authority, He must come to the Father through the Son. This acceptance is one of the fruits of conversion. While Christians are not always consistent in their recognition of God as the Voice of Authority, those who are unwilling to do so should give prayerful consideration to this question, "Have I been converted?"

The fourth implication is submission. Those who recognize God as the Voice of Authority must submit their minds to His authority. The Christian is often urged to be subject to God in every sphere of life. We are also reminded that He is Lord of our time, talents and money. Repeatedly we are reminded that our bodies and souls belong to Him. While this certainly includes the mind, how often is the mind specifically mentioned? Our minds must also be in subjection to the Lord God!

Since God is our creator and we are His creatures, every aspect of our being is His by right of creation. Because Christ, by His death upon the cross redeemed every aspect of our being, then our minds belong to Him. Since God is our sovereign and we are His subjects, our minds must also be in subjection to Him. We must recognize Him as the Voice of Authority in matters of truth and conduct and His Word as the touchstone in these realms. Since God is infinite and we are finite, let us submit our minds to His infinite wisdom and acknowledge that He alone can speak with authority concerning the mysteries of the universe and the Christian faith. The function of the mind is, not to create truth, but to discover the truths which God has revealed in nature and the Scriptures and to apply them in their proper spheres. Let us dedicate our minds to this God-given calling.

Until the mind is subject to God there is a rebel in the house. In principle, man is still in rebellion against God. While Christians are not always consistent in their submission, those who are unwilling to submit the mind to its creator and redeemer should seriously consider this question, "Do I really recognize God as the Voice of Authority?" (II Corinthians 10:3-6).

The last implication is the right to speak with certainty. Those who have accepted God as the Voice of Authority can speak with authority in realms where others may only venture an opinion.

Agnosticism is the logical consequence of accepting man as the Voice of Authority. Certainty is the logical implication of consistent Christian thinking. The Christian humbly says, "I know because the God of all wisdom and knowledge has revealed His truth and righteousness to me in nature and the Scriptures. I not only know that I am a child of God, I also know what is true and what is false, what is right and what is wrong." If you have truly accepted God as your Voice of Authority, then you may speak with authority in His name.

The Lord Jesus said, "If ye continue in my word,

then are ye my disciples indeed; and ye shall know the truth, and the truth shall make you free. If the Son therefore shall make you free, ye shall be free indeed" (John 8:31, 32, 36). In these words Christ promises those who accept Him as their Savior and are steadfast in their adherence to His standard of truth and righteousness an experiential knowledge of the truth which will make them spiritually free.

The Lord Jesus Christ is the great liberator. He frees those who believe on Him from sin's guilt and penalty, pollution and power. They are also freed from the ignorance and agnosticism which binds those for whom man is the Voice of Authority. The great emancipator has freed His people from that bondage to this end, that we might be free to follow the Voice of our Heavenly Father. Those who have been freed say with the psalmist David, "In thy light shall we see light" (Psalms 36:9). In these words they acknowledge that God is their Voice of Authority. This is an important aspect of the glorious liberty enjoyed by the children of God. This freedom is progressively gained as men apply this principle with increasing consistency in every sphere of life.

Are you in darkness and bondage or do you enjoy the freedom of those who walk in the light? Is your Voice of Authority man or God?

BIBLIOGRAPHY

Citations in this book are made from the titles listed below.

The Defense of the Faith by Cornelius Van Til (Presbyterian and Reformed Publishing Co., 1955)

Commentary on the Confession of Faith by A. A. Hodge (Presbyterian Board of Publication, Phila., 1869)

The Barthian Theology and the Man of Today by John McConnachie (Harper, New York, 1933)

Christianity Rightly So Called by Samuel G. Craig (Presbyterian and Reformed Publishing Co., 1946)

By What Standard? by Rousas J. Rushdoony (Presbyterian and Reformed Publishing Co., 1959)

Thy Word is Truth by Edward J. Young (Eerdmans Publishing Co., Grand Rapids, Mich., 1958)

Matthew Henry's Commentary (Revell, Westwood, N. J., 1959)

The Free Offer of the Gospel by John Murray and Ned B. Stonehouse (Rev. Lewis J. Grotenhuis, RFD #2, Phillipsburgh, N. J.)

Calvin's Institutes (Eerdmans)

Commentary on Romans by Charles Hodge (Eerdmans)

NOTE: For an analysis of Barth's view of the Atonement see *For Whom Did Christ Die?* by R. B. Kuiper (Eerdmans, 1959), Chapter III.